To whom do you
owe your spouse?

A Purpose-Driven Marriage

A TRIBUTE TO MY BELOVED WIFE AND BEST FRIEND
1974-2014

Wilfred R Nkoyo, Rev. (Major Retired)

WESTBOW
PRESS®
A DIVISION OF THOMAS NELSON
& ZONDERVAN

WestBow Press books may be ordered through booksellers or by contacting:

WestBow Press
A Division of Thomas Nelson & Zondervan
1663 Liberty Drive
Bloomington, IN 47403
www.westbowpress.com
1 (866) 928-1240

ISBN: 978-1-4908-9380-8 (sc)
ISBN: 978-1-4908-9381-5 (e)

Library of Congress Control Number: 2015911164

Print information available on the last page.

WestBow Press rev. date: 07/30/2015

Contents

Committed to Love and to Protect Mary to the End............................ vii

Foreword... ix

A Soldier's Obsession with Love for His Woman............................... xiii

Preface xvii

Acknowledgments...xxvii

Introduction...xxxi

Chapter 1   Meeting My High School Sweetheart 3

Chapter 2   Building a Career and a Family 23

Chapter 3   My Military Career Offers Mary a Gospel Mission Field... 26

Chapter 4   Mary's Prayers shielded me from a Certain Death
             Trap (1982–84)... 35

Chapter 5   They Come to Our Home to Kill to Steal and to
             Destroy but find a Heavenly Host Waiting to Resist....... 49

Chapter 6   By Faith Mary Pursues Our Preordained Inheritance...... 77

Chapter 7   Opening New Doors of Opportunity (2011 to Present)... 105

Chapter 8   A General Who Marched on to the End In
             Defiance of Infirmities... 115

Epilogue..131

Appendix 133

A Pictorial Story of Family in Phases Courtship, Marriage,
Parenting and Grand parenting..149

About the Author 213

Committed to Love and to Protect Mary to the End

Mary had adoring eyes for the man she loved and wholly trusted, and this admiration intensified with time to the end. The angelic girl whom I had first seen that night in high school was now mine at last to have, to hold, to love, and to protect. And, as symbolized by the arc of swords on the cover, I was committed to protect her from physical harm with my own life, to shield her from emotional traumas, and to foster her spiritual excellence; committed to uphold her dignity, honor, and respect by all; committed to trust her judgments, decisions, motives, intentions, and counsel to me, and to the end, committed to love, to cherish, to desire, and to admire her daily in sickness or in health until death did us part and so the reason, my own portrait is embedded on her gravestone and my future grave by hers to signify commitment to Mary beyond her earthly life.

Foreword

Writing a foreword for this book—a tribute to the late Rev. Mary Nkoyo, intended also to empower marriage commitments and positive parenting—gives me immense pride and is a unique privilege.

My relationship with Mary and Wilfred Nkoyo dates back to high school days—forty years ago as of June 2014 when Mary passed. I was extremely happy to be admitted to Nyandarua High School after passing my Kenya certificate of primary education. My joy was short-lived when I realized I faced a group of students who had just graduated from form one and were now ready to "welcome" us to take their place. The bullying that accompanied this "welcome" of new students was done discretely so that the teachers and prefects would not know. However, the greeting sometimes became so violent that students would end up being expelled from school. I was not spared from this blustering and intimidation.

Two beautiful girls approached me and said, "Hi, you mono. You are going to wash our two blouses." The girls had just finished using a curling iron, and their white blouses were covered with grease and dirt. I had to use my soap to do the job. That did not sit well with me, but since I feared a beating, I obliged. A few days passed and the two girls came again with the same demand. This time I did not say anything but took the blouses, put them in the sink, and reported the two girls to the house captain. They were punished. They never repeated that stunt again. One of those girls was Mary Mbuthuri, later Mary Nkoyo. Though she had not yet been saved, she was a star with beauty, elegance, and brains.

Two years down the line, we became birds of the same feather. Mary and I had accepted the Lord as our Savior, and we were now in the same Christian union. We had forgiven each other and had moved on to become good friends.

Not long after that, a handsome young Maasai man named Wilfred Nkoyo entered our school for advanced-level classes. He came swinging a guitar and singing for Jesus without apology. He was an instant attraction for everyone. Mary and Wilfred were active members of our Christian union at the school and that involvement brought them close enough, giving Mary greater advantage over other female admirers. They were most of the time seen together around school. After graduation from high school, the relationship between them blossomed into marriage. The high school sweethearts were now husband and wife.

After we all relocated to the United States, our communication was revitalized. Caroline, their daughter, would sometimes visit our home after she entered Baylor University in Waco, Texas, in 1999. My husband— Pastor Kingori—and I had many opportunities to interact more closely with the Nkoyos after they came down to Texas in 2001. Their love for each other was exemplary. They were together most of the time. You would think they were newlyweds. Our church, Neema Gospel Church, had the honor of hosting them as speakers to our couples on several occasions. The Nkoyos were very resourceful. They were also there to celebrate many church milestones with us.

On June 4, 2014, the Rev. Mary Nkoyo, my friend and big sister, was promoted to glory. My heart was devastated yet I mourned with hope because I knew she had gone to meet her Master, whom she served with single-minded focus and dedication.

One thing that stood out about Mary was the fire of God in her. She still had the passion and tenacity of the "guerrillas for Christ," an evangelistic movement that took Kenya by storm during the '70s revivals. Zeal for the Father's work consumed her. She sent monthly devotions and calendars to our addresses with her own postage. She loved to worship at every opportunity.

Mary was an ordained minister and founded the International Prayer Network ministry under the auspices of Christian Heritage Ministries International Inc., founded by her and her husband. She coordinated prayer meetings, christened "Standing in the Gap," for individuals, families, and nations.

Another thing that stood out about Mary was her spirit of excellence and distinction. She was always elegant in her dress and her presentation. She knew how to adorn herself like royalty. Her colors were always organized and coordinated. She did everything with a sense of perfection. I never once saw Mary sloppily dressed. Her meeting rooms were nicely arranged and decorated. The food was classic and delicious. Mary was also very generous.

Mary struggled with health issues toward the end of her life, but she stood strong even when she faced severe challenges with her deteriorating condition. She remained steadfast in faith and never talked about her weakened health. She was always positive, always tenacious, always standing on the promises of God for healing. There were times when we thought Mary would not last a month, but she would bounce back and stay with us a little longer.

Major Nkoyo stood by Mary's side during these challenging periods. The way he stayed with his wife in her time of great need is a lesson for all couples. People go to the altar during a wedding and proclaim "for better or for worse, for richer or poorer, in sickness and in health" without stopping to think what those words mean. Many a times we never consider their weight until reality knocks on our door. It has been a great privilege to know the Nkoyos, a couple who fought the good fight, ran the race, and kept the faith all the way to "death do us part."

This book will challenge you to look at your marriage as stewardship with an eternal purpose and will highlight the entities that have a stake in your marriage. These entities count on the strength and soundness of your marriage and would suffer untold loss if it fell apart. This danger calls for deliberate stewardship of your marriage as an institution that God has ordained. This possibility should also strengthen your resolve to endure the many challenges and contradictions confronting marriage in this generation.

God has a stake in your marriage. He is glorified when a marriage is thriving. Your children also have a stake in your marriage. Your spouse means the world to your children. There is a place for both parents in the hearts of their children. Disintegration of a marriage causes the children to be fearful, insecure, and oftentimes depressed. Your relatives on either side also have a stake in your union. A stable marriage is a sanctuary for family members from both sides. Cohesion of the family is undoubtedly a great blessing to the extended family. Friends provide needed spice to a marriage. They usually will treat you and your spouse as a unit, and disintegration of that unity would cause them to scatter. If your union broke down, they would get confused in choosing their allegiances.

Once you come to terms with the fact that you owe your spouse to all these entities, you will be conscious of treating your spouse with the utmost respect and care. You will also be determined to contend for your union regardless of the challenges that may afflict it. You will be equipped to fight the good fight; you will run your race until death parts you from your spouse.

I strongly recommend this book to those on the path to getting married, those already married, and those who may want to counsel or assist married couples facing challenges.

—Lucy N. Kingori, Associate Pastor, Neema Gospel Church,
Dallas, Texas

A Soldier's Obsession
with Love for His Woman

I don't know where to start or where to end when it comes to our sister Mary. She was indeed a special woman of God, a dear sister in the Lord, and a true friend. I met Mary more than thirty-six years ago when we were single girls in Nairobi, Kenya. I was working for World Vision International at the Kenya Re Building while Mary was working at Bima House for the Kenya Insurance Company. We used to attend lunch-hour prayer meetings together, and in doing that, we built a strong bond of fellowship and I became part of her network of friends. In October 1979 I had the privilege of being a bridesmaid in Mary's wedding, a colorful military ceremony in Narok. This was the first time I had been in a military wedding, and I was proud to have participated. It remains vivid in my memory even after thirty-six years.

An intriguing encounter that took place in my office in Kenya around 1986 has also remained embedded in my memory. Few of the Nkoyos' friends may know about this incident, which illustrates how far Wilfred's obsession with loving Mary could go. For the record and for the glory of God, I take the liberty to share the story here. Mary went missing from Narok, her husband's hometown, about a hundred miles from the Gilgil barracks where Wilfred was stationed. She had been in Narok supervising work on a family project but had grown exhausted and had taken off on a three-day prayer retreat with a women's group (of which the Rev. Anne Muthama was part) in Nairobi about ninety miles away. Neither her husband nor those around her, including her babysitter, were privy to this move. As a woman of prayer, she wanted time alone with a few praying women friends.

When her husband learned that Mary was missing and that she was last seen hitching a ride to Nairobi in an unknown vehicle, he fell into a wild frenzy. He was shocked because his faithful wife was his closest confidante, and this kind of thing had never happened before in their seven years of marriage, not even during their diplomatic service in the United States. Mary had also chosen not to use the family car that she always used to get around. Major Nkoyo learned the news about his missing wife soon after arriving at his base in Gilgil following a field exercise. Dressed in his military camouflage with a squad of similarly dressed soldiers, he hastily left Gilgil on a Friday afternoon in his camouflage command jeep, heading for Nairobi. He determined that this city was the place to start the search for his wife, whom he feared could be held hostage there.

Since I was their closest friend, strategically located and with good communication, Wilfred decided I should assist in the search. That is how I found myself facing a nearly hysterical soldier searching for the woman he idolized. That evening I had stayed late at the office and was finishing an assignment when suddenly I heard a knock at my door. When I opened it, a soldier stepped into the room. He was in full jungle camouflage uniform. He looked frantic and was breathing hard. I did not recognize him at first because I was gripped with fear and confusion. Standing before me was an unfamiliar wild soldier, not the harmless and calm person I had always called Brother Major Nkoyo. Before we could exchange our normal "Praise the Lord" greetings and pleasantries, he looked straight at me with a soldier's unblinking eyes and inquired if I had seen or heard from his wife. That question added to my trauma as I imagined the worst for Mary.

Wilfred knew of my friendship with Mary and of our extensive network of friends, and from my office he knew he could easily reach many contacts. That was why he came to me first, but his question and the narrative that followed amplified my shock. I feared that my beloved sister's life was in danger. Wilfred said Mary had gone missing from her home in Narok either Thursday or that morning, and he feared that she could be held hostage in Nairobi and might already be badly harmed or at the mercy of her tormentors. My assignment was to call every emergency ward and morgue in the city to describe Mary and to find out whether such a person had been admitted dead or alive. Then I was to call relatives and family friends to check whether she had been seen. My office turned into an operations and command center, and I was the chief of the operations, taking orders from an incensed and impatient operations commander. Stated in military fashion, my mission was to make phone calls and to locate Mary dead or alive. And that is what I did, putting aside my other assignment.

I will never forget the power and the passion of this obsessed lover, worried that his only woman could have innocently fallen into a trap set by people whom she blindly trusted. This was the man I had always known as a gentle brother in Christ, but that evening I feared he was ready and willing to hurt anyone causing the disappearance of his wife or doing her harm. There was also a hint that he was not alone. My suspicions were confirmed when on our way out I saw that he had a squad of soldiers waiting outside in his official Jeep. He also told me that matatu touts responsible for Mary's fuzzy travel arrangements in an unknown vehicle with a male driver had been locked up in Narok police cells.

As I made call after call, the animated soldier could not stand still, but kept pacing the floor and breathing heavily. Most see such stories only in wild-west movies or in romance novels. Crazed with love for a woman who has vanished mysteriously, an armed lover is set to burn down towns, start wars, and destroy everything in his wrath. I saw this live in my office when I found myself with a soldier searching for his missing woman. Unfortunately, that evening we did not find any helpful leads, adding to the mystery, but that was not the end, only the beginning.

I later learned that the following day Wilfred moved to a strategic spot on the Rift Valley escarpment, a narrow section of the main highway to his hometown, and set up a roadblock. He and his soldiers then stopped every matatu (public transport vehicle) coming into and out of Narok to inquire about and check for Mary. This was a surprise to matatu operators, who were unfamiliar with military roadblocks.

It was here on the third day that Wilfred finally found his Mary in the back seat of a matatu, returning home from her retreat in Nairobi. She was surprised to see him but not afraid because to her he was not a soldier but a loving husband who never hurt or threatened her or raised his voice at her no matter what. But to see him looking ragged, fatigued, and worried for her made Mary feel sorry that it had to come to this. When their eyes met as she sat calmly in the back of the vehicle, Wilfred briefly became emotional but quickly regained his composure. He walked back slowly to where she sat and without saying anything, lovingly and gently reached out and took her hand like a child's and hugged her. Then, hand in hand, they slowly left the vehicle to the amazement of the passengers and the driver. Wilfred helped Mary into a waiting Jeep, and off they went straight back to the Gilgil barracks more than fifty miles away.

Wilfred's driver and the rest of the soldiers were surprised that there was no bitter exchange between the couple. At Gilgil, in the privacy of their military mansion, Mary opened up to her husband about the emotional, spiritual, and physical stress that the Narok project had placed on her and about her need for quiet prayer. She had no way of reaching him while away in the field.

That was the beginning of the end of the couple's interest in Narok, their dream project, the "Crystal Mall," and any involvements that would separate them. Because Major Nkoyo would often be assigned duties in the field, away from his family, he took early retirement from the military in 1988.

I have found it prudent to share this story and what decades of close fellowship brought me to know about the Nkoyos to illustrate a loving commitment between a husband and a wife. They never allowed material gain, social status, ill health, valleys, or mountains to separate them until death did indeed part them after thirty-five years of marriage. Revelation 2:10 reminds us to be faithful to the end. The Nkoyos were an exemplary story of enduring faithfulness and affinity for each other. It is no wonder that this love-obsessed soldier would act so crazy when his woman could not be found.

Love is contagious, growing and multiplying, and Mary was herself obsessed with love for her husband. The woman had a strong attachment to him that started in their years of courtship. After they got married, she was always sitting by his side. This explains why that brief glitch, when Mary momentarily went off of his radar, caused Wilfred such anxiety and frenzy. I am proud and privileged to share this story and with my late husband and our children to have been associated with such a loving couple, who also loved the brethren.

—Mary Gathunguri, Baltimore, Maryland, USA

Preface

This book is dedicated to you, my beloved children, Caroline and Armstrong, to your wonderful spouses, and to the greatest gift God has added to me: my adorable grandchildren Tumaini and John and all others who will come after them. I love you all and always will. Each of you means the world to me. In this book I will remind you how to live in harmony with one another, to love one another, and to respect others who may be different from you, a secret to winning and influencing people for the kingdom of God and one by which your mother and I lived. My central message is this: discover entities who will give purpose to your marriage commitment and enhance it.

Though neither your blood sister nor your blood brother, from my experience, your spouse is closer than either and should always come first, ahead of every other person in your life including your mother, your father, and even your children. None of these should come between you and your spouse because in the end when they are gone from your life only your spouse will remain standing by you. And when the storms of life arrive, your best ally should be your spouse. That was the case in my life with your mother from the day we got married. Only God, the creator of each of you, should come before your spouse. He comes to unite and not to divide you. God will never be a competitor in your marriage relationship. He wants to enhance your union.

I write this at a time when many couples are choosing divorce as the easy way out of normal family challenges or after allowing outside forces, including relatives and friends, to take control and to influence their lives, thus undermining their unions. I said normal challenges because in every family there will always be crises, and these are normal. But today many couples walk away from each other over petty issues rather than work on them, hoping they can escape life's realities by finding someone else who may be less problematic and may be wealthier, prettier, healthier, or more easygoing. All these are temporal fantasies, but when the shaking comes, only the permanent will remain. Your spouse is and should be your permanent ally and confidant.

In sharing some of our marriage experiences, both highs and lows, I hope that you will learn lessons that will help you find meaning and purpose to keep your marriage commitment strong in times of crises. And as sure as the sun will rise tomorrow, crises will come. That shaking must happen at some point in your marriage. My objective is to help you identify entities that will give purpose and define clearly why you must remain true to your marriage commitment after everything and everybody have gone. That discovery energized me, making me determined and unmovable in resisting the health problems that for more than twenty years worked relentlessly against my relationship with your mother. These conditions might have undermined our marriage, but in the end my love for your mother got even stronger, giving us thirty-five great years of commitment to one another. As you will discover in my narration, you as our children became one of those entities that added greatly to our purpose, strengthening that commitment.

GOD AS THE NUMBER-ONE ENTITY

If you let God become the number-one entity, He will open your eyes to see and appreciate the other vital entities and to remain accountable to them. And when life's challenges come, whether physical, social, psychological, emotional, spiritual, or economic, these entities will never leave you to struggle alone. They will become your trusted allies, inspiring and encouraging you in the face of life's storms. By recognizing and appreciating the contribution of these entities to the well-being of your relationship, you will find strength and purpose in your union and your marriage commitment will remain strong. They will inspire you to ride on the storms. Surfers ride on the waves for enjoyment, and you can do the same. You can turn storms into opportunities and rise to greatness, as some of my stories will show.

As an aviator, I learned something interesting about aerodynamics. Even the largest and heaviest jets when taking off must run head-on against the wind.. In the same way, we must use the storms in life to help us rise to the destinations of our dreams. God allows these storms as opportunities to rise. That is how we ended up in America, the most stable and surest land of opportunities. By storms He brought us out and through storms He sustained us. Remember always to make God the number-one entity in your lives.

MARY'S MERITS AS AN ENTITY

In this book I will tell you intriguing stories about my experiences with your mother, who never ceased to be that mystic girl I first saw in high school. We met in May 1974 as teenagers in high school and fell head over heels in love. The two of us became inseparable, though we had nothing to share apart from our utopian dreams. We both came from underprivileged families that could afford only our one-way bus fare to school. We had no pocket money and had to wait for the return bus fare at the end of the term.

Your mother and I were in courtship for five long but worthwhile years, waiting to marry partly because we were students and partly because I had to graduate from military college and settle down in my new army career. We got married in October 1979 when I was twenty-five and a full lieutenant in the army. Mary was twenty three. For the next thirty-five years, whether in plenty or with just enough, the passionate love between us bridged the difference. Though in her last twenty one years she was physically frail and mentally foggy at times as she struggled with depression and later with kidney disease, my adoring love for my high school sweetheart only intensified, prevailing over her circumstances, and my commitment to our covenant got stronger with each challenge. I felt as if no other woman existed on earth. She was my queen and I made it known to all.

The mystic in my high school sweetheart held sway over me until the day I laid her in her grave. I chose to have mine beside hers and my picture embedded on the granite as a clear reminder to all and sundry who Mary belonged to both in life and in death. In the forty years of our life together, I treasured and shielded no one more than Mary. Though she is gone physically, her investment in my life and the values she added to me and to our family remains forever. Think of your spouses along such lines, always seeing them as entities who will bring unique and lasting values and benefits to your lives, even if just one value.

I will attempt to show you the values and benefits that Mary added to you and me. No woman could have influenced and impacted every sphere of my life so powerfully or in the same way. Her merits in this regard will be evident throughout this book, story after story showing how her sensitivity to the "still small voice" of God opened doors of victory and prosperity. And how her courage and boldness locked out enemies of our progress as a family, to the extent of saving us from certain death and destruction. You and I and generations to come will remain debtors to your mother. You can repay her for all she did only by doing what I tried to do all my life for her: to love and honor your spouses and to remain committed to the covenant you made on the day you said "I do till death do part" no matter what.

I learned to regard my wife as my equal, never viewing her as a weaker vessel or gender. In times of crisis, after I had called upon God, Mary was the first human ally I sought, and she could always count on me in all matters. Mary and I ascended and descended ladders hand in hand and celebrated each other's rise in status while providing each other a safe landing cushion, as you will see. On matters of contentment in life, we were well taught in Scripture: "I know what it is to be in need, and I know what it is to have plenty. I have learned the secret of being content in any and every situation, whether well fed or hungry, whether living in plenty or in want" (Philippians 4:12 NIV).

Mary fulfilled me. She was all the woman I needed, wanted and desired and so was I the total man to her as expressed variously in her words. She also made up for my shortcomings and in turn I did hers. Nobody could fault Mary because to me Mary was always right even when wrong. She made me complete and so did I make her. We were content and happy living small in a hut or living large in mansions, sleeping on the floor or in king-size beds (these extremes were true experiences in our lives). I am forever indebted to Mary for making me feel loved and for affirming my self-worth in all situations from the day we met in high school to her last breath forty years later.

My children as an entity

The other important entities were each of you. I was convinced that my children deserved a mother, secure in the love and commitment of a husband she could trust and love so in turn she could have the capacity to love and trust you. Aggravated, disrespected, violated, humiliated, publicly shamed, and neglected mothers; a wife who must daily have to compete for attention with other women in her husband's life, vent their anger and frustration through their innocent children. The same is true of husbands similarly treated and cheated on by their wives. Such spouses have no love or trust in their hearts to share or show to their children and lack patience necessary to cope with challenges facing their own developing children. They are like dry wells to their thirsty children and are always high strung and high handed in dealing with them on petty issues.

I wanted your mother to tenderly love and fully trust you, and so I had to build that capacity in her by tenderly loving and fully trusting her. I would respect, honor, and nourish her to the overflow, physically, emotionally, and spiritually, publicly and privately. I had to make her know, whispering in her ear and looking her strait in the eye when we were just by ourselves and telling the "whole" world, in her presence who she was and what she meant to me. She often bragged to her friends, men and women alike, of how her husband loved and trusted her. That was made possible with God's help and a deliberate decision to do so. Scripture says, "Husbands, love your wives, just as Christ loved the church and gave himself up for her" (Ephesians 5:25 NIV). That was my guiding verse. With my part done, I was sure Mary would do her part from the overflow: to love and trust you as I did love and trust her. She adored you and your spouses and trusted your judgments and counsel to the day she died.

I owed you a mother whom you would always find waiting at the doorstep with open arms and a broad smile, saying, "I love you, my child. Welcome home." I wanted you to have a mother who would confidently and authoritatively admonish you and counsel you when it became necessary but never to use demeaning and insulting language or physically assault you. Most important, I wanted her to respect you, especially in the presence of your friends. That is why you never learned even one curse word or mean gestures in dealing with others no matter how much they aggravated you. Your mother encouraged you to rise to greatness and praised your smallest efforts. That is the mother I owed you and by God's grace, gave you.

In equal measure, your mother faithfully, humbly, and adoringly loved and honored me in private and in public. Mary repaid me love for love and trust for trust. She did that despite my shortcomings, choosing to love me for everything I was and everything I was not. She loved me in spite of my imperfections. In a generation where wives and husbands call each other by their first names, your mom went to her grave still passionately addressing me as "my beloved, my love, and father of my children." I addressed her in the same passionate language and respect. She brought honor to me and made me the envy of many who may have been more prosperous and of higher status. Some, especially in my years in the military, became envious of me for her beauty, decency and elegance to the point of planning to hurt me. Your mother always addressed me with respect, not because she feared me or was intimidated by me but because she loved and trusted me. She never second-guessed my commitment to her well-being or to our covenant.

Finally, my desire in writing this book is to encourage you to remain committed to the covenant that you made before God and in the presence of many witnesses on the day you said "I do." Learn from us. We are your best example, and you in turn can be the best examples to your children. Your children will always need and deserve a father and a mother, not a deserted and singled parent. My daily prayer and desire, which was always your mother's to the end, is that you will remain true to your spouse. You can never walk away from the covenant without hurting someone: yourself first, your spouse, your children, and me among many other stakeholders to whom you owe your marriage. Remember that your marriage is not yours alone. Others have interests in it, with God as the chief stakeholder.

If you determine in your hearts to honor and glorify God through your marriage commitment, everything else will fall into place. That was my determination in a journey that lasted thirty-five years and that ended only when I crossed the final bridge called death-do-part. Your mother and I walked hand in hand, sometimes up the mountains of glamour and high dreams and at other times down into the lowest valleys of gloom and uncertainty. However, no power on earth could separate us or diminish our commitment and our love for each other. No woman, no relative, no material things could rise to the level of my love for Mary. And for this, I give credit to the entities in total who gave purpose to my love and to my marriage commitment to your mother.

My beloved daughter Caroline, you opened the womb of a great mother. Learn from her life, a life you witnessed. Your mother loved and trusted me and was always faithful to me. As I have always urged you, in whatever circumstances you may find yourselves and whatever the differences between you and your spouse, be the first to show honor, humility, and respect for your husband. Love him always and remain faithful to the marriage commitment between you. You are your husband's keeper, never to let or encourage him to associate himself with dubious individuals taking part in risky activities that you sense or know for a fact could expose him to indignity, disrepute, ridicule, lawbreaking, physical harm or likely to harm others.

It is your duty to protect your husband. That might sound controlling, but the truth is that men, more often than women are vulnerable to manipulation and exploitation for a simple reason: women have superior and sharper intuition. Over the years, your mom used that superiority to keep me out of trouble, and I guarantee that you will never be wrong if you do this for your husband because you will help him and your family in the same way. Your mother was my confidante; she had my ear, and I had hers. She would never allow me to enter into a deal or to confide in a stranger, a family member, or a family friend without her involvement and privy to all the details. Men are headliners, but women can read fine print and hidden clauses. She had the boldness to counsel me out of bad deals however sweet they sounded. She did this wisely, working around my stubbornness (as you well know how stubborn I can get at times, and so is your husband). That is how she kept me out of trouble for the thirty-five years of our union. Be your husband's keeper behind the scenes without apology but respectfully. Remember always to let your husband shine. Make him admired by all and help him to live out his full potential. Never, never, never, scold your husband in public or in the presence of your children no matter what. If you want to be his queen, start by making him your king. That was your mother's secret.

Always remember that your husband is my other son and the father of my beloved grandchildren. You owe him to them and to me.

Likewise, my son Armstrong, love your wife in the same way I loved your mother. You witnessed my undivided love and attention for her and how I always did my best to protect her from physical or emotional harm. She could never complain that I had an eye on another woman, because there was never another. Not because there were no other fairer looking women but because there was only one Mary. God never makes duplicates. That was true going back to the days she was only my girlfriend. Your mother was always number one and the only woman (wife) in my life. Never expose your wife to indignity, ridicule or competition with other women (including your sister or mother if she was still alive). Let her remain the queen of your life, your ultimate counsel in all matters of family life just as your mom was to me. If let your wife's counsel prevail on family matters, whenever things don't work out as expected, she will take part of the responsibility. In other words, never ignore her advice and opinion.

If you let your wife partake in all your family decisions, let her be your spokesperson there will be no room left for others especially strange women to interfere with your relationship. Even manipulative males will be kept at bay because they will know whom they must contend with before getting to you. I discovered this over the years by learning to read subliminal messages your mother would send me when in the company of our female friends or male associates. She communicated her comforts and discomforts through body language, mainly her eyes, and I could quickly decipher when she was saying, "It's our time to leave the scene. I am getting uncomfortable." She made a habit of standing or sitting next to me during public occasions to shield me, to the point of stepping secretly on my toes, squeezing firmly on my hand (to which she often held) or looking straight in my eye saying, "do not commit". Many wise ladies do that because they care for their husbands and families. They respond by asking for more time to consider the offer.

Avoid playing hide-and-seek games with your wife. Always be open with her, especially when engaging in a conversation with your mutual female friends. Always conclude the engagement with them in her presence. No private follow-ups. Your wife is my other daughter and the mother of very important biological extensions of me, my grandchildren. You owe a mother to them and a daughter to me. My son, you are my pride. You are the biological extension of me. I see a reflection of me in you in the way you do certain things every day even though we wrestle over issues, ideas, and dreams, sometimes agreeing to disagree with a handshake. Your successes are my successes and so are your failures mine.

Acknowledgments

As the 2013 began, Mary and I started considering how we could bring together couples of our generation in what we would call the Thirty-Plus Open Forum. In an effort to encourage one another, couples married for thirty years or more would come together occasionally and share their practical experiences in the four phases of family life-cycle: during courtship, marriage, parenting and grand parenting, sharing their challenges and how they handled each situation. All in all, bringing Christian couples together to celebrate God's idea of family at a time when counterfeit marriage ideas and myriads of counter-marriage forces have taken center stage.

The idea never came to fruition, because in 2014, Mary's health started deteriorating. But after she passed and the Lord laid it upon my heart to write this multi-purpose tribute to her, I asked our longtime couple friends to write a few lines of endorsement. Most of the couples responding had been married for more than thirty years. Each revisited the low and high moments of our experiences together as if to say, "We are the critical mass for the Thirty-Plus Forum that will bring about a revival of faith in the institution of marriage and encourage positive parenting."

In an opening salvo, Pastor Lucy Kingori, a powerful woman of God, has penned a historical foreword for this book. She takes us back more than forty years to a wilderness named Mary Mbuthuri in a place called Nyandarua High School. In this wilderness a no-nonsense little tigress ruled. It was either her way or no way. These were the BC, or "Before Christ," years of Mary Mbuthuri's life.

Enter Dr. Mary Murimi, who during those revival times was a hitchhiking student-preacher. She had no known income apart from pocket money from Papa, but in her arsenal was the mighty lion of Judah. She declared war on the tigress and seized the wilderness, converting it into a productive land for the Lord's kingdom for the next forty-one years. That accounts for the AD, or "After Christ," years of Mary Mbuthuri's life.

Next, the Rev. Anne Nyambura Muthama reveals to us the seeds of the latter-day ministries led by her and the Rev. Mary Nkoyo, how and where they were laid, watered, and germinated. It began in a room shared by the two single girls off of Shilingi Road in Nairobi, Kenya. For the first time we learn of the Beyond Kitchen ministry, which was never registered, even though they lacked theological training, the two single girls, under the influence of the Holy Ghost, went out and about spreading the gospel and reaping souls for the Kingdom.

The Rev. Wambui Njoroge shares a unique and intriguing encounter with a single-minded woman in Washington, D.C., who chose to leave behind all the glitter and niceties of America, the ultimate dream destination for many, for the sake of her marriage, returning home with her children to the muddy rural trails of Kenya to reunite with the only man she loved. In making this choice, we see how Mary valued marriage and family over material things.

The Rev. Dr. James and Margret Njoroge tell a moving story of their beloved son, who had become vulnerable in Virginia. Relying on their long-term friendship, they asked the Nkoyos down in Texas to take him in and to provide him refuge and counsel in a new environment. This turned out to be the best decision they made and testified to Mary's generosity and benevolence. She would open her home as a retreat for couples, families, and individuals and that explains why she opened her home in Limuru Kenya to human angels divinely send to save her family from death.

We read story after story by highly accomplished and successful Christian couples and leaders and their stories seem to come from the same epistle: Dr. Wilson and Mrs. Elizabeth Wamani, Brig. (retired) Phillip and Mrs. Martha Chebbet, Mr. Duncan and Mrs. Asenath Gichia, Rev. Phillip and Rev. Rebecca Mwonga, Rev. Ronni and Rev. Kim Holmes (the Nkoyo family's pastors in Waco), Maj. (Retired) and Mrs. Rose Njiru, and Mrs. Mary Gathunguri (author of "A soldier's obsession with love of his woman").

This book would not have been possible without the kind contributions of these credible witnesses to the life and times of the Rev. Mary Nkoyo and her husband Major Nkoyo as an exemplary couple. Innumerable couples, privy to the purpose of this book strongly encouraged me to provide this tool for the empowerment of marriages and for positive parenting.

To all the above, my greatest appreciation and gratitude for making this tribute to Mary and this timely message to couples and parents possible.

Maj. (Retired) Rev. Wilfred Nkoyo
For the Nkoyo family

Introduction

DEFINING THE TITLE AND THE ENTITIES

The title of this book is a question, and in the answers lie the secret to longevity and the driving purpose for your marriage commitment. The question is, "To whom do you owe your spouse?" Put in another way, when the going gets tough and storms arise in your relationship, who or what will motivate a recommitment to your marriage covenant? When the winds blow and you are about to let go, what will you grasp to keep from giving up? As a steward of your marriage commitment, to whom are you accountable? Who else do you consider a stakeholder, a person having a vested interest in the way you treat your spouse whether in private or public?

Besides you, could there be other people who may have even greater stakes in your spouse and in your stewardship? If you seriously start seeking answers to the primary question, "To whom do you owe your spouse?" you will discover not one, not two, but several entities to whom you are indebted. These entities count on the strength of your union and would suffer untold loss if it fell apart. Such entities give a meaningful and enduring purpose to your union and provide reasons to be a good steward of your marriage. They will perpetually give you power to overcome many challenges to your marriage relationship, thus adding to its longevity.

An article on the Christian website http://christianpf.com/stewardship/ defines *stewardship* as "the conducting, supervising, or managing of something; especially: the careful and responsible management of something entrusted to one's care; for example, stewardship of our natural resources." How many spouses today see themselves as managers of their partners, and such partners as something entrusted to their care by someone else? How many spouses take into account the interests of other parties in their partners? All too often spouses use the self-centered expressions "This is my wife" or "This is my husband." This gives rise to the attitude that says, "What I do with or to my husband/wife is nobody's business." We rely on the same idea when referring to property: "This is my car, my house, my food, my dog, my cat, my cow." We simply add a wife or a husband to the list.

However, there are other stakeholders in your union, and they have vested interests in your stewardship of your spouse, specifically in the way you treat the person. You are therefore indebted to them. Some of these stakeholders have greater vested interests in your spouse than you do. First, there is the creator of your spouse. Your partner is God's child and not your child! Your wife is not your baby girl neither is your husband your baby boy. As the Scripture says, "So God created man in his own image, in the image of God created he him; male and female created he them" (Genesis 1:27 KJV). Second, your spouse is an entity who has contributed in many ways to your life and to whom you are indebted. Third, your children are an entity. Your spouse is their father or mother and would mean the world to them regardless of his or her social, economic, emotional, or physical status. Fourth, your spouse has relatives, entities to whom you owe his/her wellbeing. Fifth, there are your mutual friends. They have stakes in your union as a couple and in each of you, and you owe your spouse to them.

Once you can clearly identify the entities to whom you owe your spouse and to whom you are accountable, you will start viewing yourself as your spouse's keeper, a steward entrusted with the care of something precious to these entities. You will then begin respecting the entities' interests and as a result will develop a greater appreciation of your spouse and will place more value on this person. Your marriage relationship and your commitment to your covenant will have a driving purpose. Your constant consciousness of the entities will make them tangible anchors and shock absorbers, and no matter what trials, temptations, or storms life may hurl at you, your marriage commitment will remain strong.

Sometimes in your relationship, life will be sweet. Everything will look beautiful, and you will agree on almost every issue. Your children will make the right choices, get good grades in school, and be respectful to you, and the family will enjoy great health and wealth. That is a mountaintop experience. But at other times, there will be deep and treacherous valleys to cross. Nothing will work as planned or expected, and you will be unable to agree on anything. Instead, you and your spouse will trade blame for decisions that did not work out. Your children will make bad choices, get poor grades, and become oppositional at home. Health issues will drain your savings, and you will have difficulties at work or may even be laid off with no reliable income.

But whether you are atop a mountain or in a treacherous valley, as long as you recognize that higher driving purpose born out of indebtedness to each other and to other entities, your marriage commitment will remain constant no matter what happens around you. As long as you are conscious that you owe your spouse to some entity beyond your selfish interests, an entity whom you respect, honor, and care about and to whom you are accountable regarding your marriage relationship, you will go to any length to nurture that relationship and to make your marriage work.

The entities mentioned above, who will feature prominently in this book, brought strength, motivation, and inspiration to my marriage commitment to Mary, giving it unshakable purpose to the last moment of our thirty-five years together—from October 13, 1979, the day I said "I do," to June 4, 2014, the day death parted us.

The last twenty-one years of our marriage were particularly treacherous and stressful oftentimes we had to deal with Mary's recurring episodes of depression. The last five were the most complicated and tricky, since depression more often than not got in the way of treating Mary's terminal kidney disease, diagnosed at the end of 2009. There was no doubt Mary would not survive or live long enough unless she was willing to be regularly dialyzed. She cooperated as long as she stayed on her antidepressants. But when she relapsed into depression after secretly discontinuing the antidepressants, she would refuse to be dialyzed, denying that she was depressed or suffering kidney failure. According to American law, she could not be medicated or treated against her will without due judicial process to prove that she was depressed and that her life was in imminent danger.

My number one responsibility was to keep track of Mary's consistency in taking her medications, especially her antidepressants, and to order refills, but because I could not directly supervise her intake, I would sometimes discover too late that she had discontinued her medication and reached a point of no return. That was always a sad discovery considering the turn-around time and the complex process involved in getting her back on track. The part I played in having Mary involuntarily hospitalized often made me her "enemy" and betrayer. The person she most trusted and idolized all her adult life, seemingly having turned against her. Those are the only rare moments I saw Mary weep as she looked at me with same adoring eyes. She made me weep while trying to hide my tears to show tough love and strenght but as I drove behind the vehicle conveying her, I would cry loudly in the privacy of our car as the image of a crying Mary flashed in my eyes. Details of such episodes are covered in another part of this book.

The most rewarding feeling for me always came at the end of each turn-around, which would take more than a year. Then I would see my queen reborn, my bride, my pride, and my closest friend at her very best, not only functioning at full capacity as the "best mom in the whole world" (Armstrong's description when he was twelve) but also as the most articulate minister of the gospel, flowing in prophecy, word of knowledge, burst in laughter, dance and a song of praise. I would listen quietly as she offered a prayer full of faith that shook the gates of hell. Then I would remember the Scripture: "Wherefore take unto you the whole armour of God that ye may be able to withstand in the evil day, and having done all, to stand" (Ephesians 6:13 KJV). I did all for Mary in the knowledge that I owed her to other entities. To whom do you owe your spouse? How far can you go when they most need you. What gives purpose to your marriage commitment?

ENTITIES KEEP THE FIRE BURNING EVEN AFTER ALL PHYSICAL GLORY HAS FADED

When good looks and physical strength fade, will the anchor of your commitment hold? Your spouse's attractive appearance will vanish and vision will grow dim because these things are temporary. A time will come when your spouse cannot find his or her way around the house; memory will become foggy even unable to recall your name; physical abilities will be reduced and sexual drive will become history. Personal resources may dwindle to a trickle, but your commitment can remain strong to the end as long as it stays anchored in the entities you have identified depending on their permanency (like the examples shared earlier) and to whom you are obligated. The ship may be torn by tempests of time, but the anchor will still hold. In what is your commitment anchored? Is it the permanent or the temporal? What purposes drive your marriage?

ENTITIES WORK IN YOU IN MOMENTS OF CRISES, HELPING YOU TO REFLECT ON PAST VICTORIES

The debt you owe to a person whom you hold in high esteem becomes a priority obligation in your budget. You will go to great lengths to make sure the payments are made on time and without fail—even if you have to borrow from somewhere else, essentially digging a hole to fill a more important one. Your love for your spouse will remain strong despite your partner's shortcomings or health challenges, external pressures, and temptations as long as you determine that you owe that spouse to entities whom you hold high in esteem. For example, if you see God as the ultimate entity who drew you together for His divine purposes, you're your goal and desire will be to glorify Him through your commitment to the marriage covenant n matter what. And before you can open your mouth to spew ugly words at your spouse for not meeting your expectations, your desire to honor God will shut your mouth up.

Images of your children, your relatives, and your friends—entities you have chosen to honor with your marriage and to whom you consider yourself indebted—will flash a red light in your mind. Some will confront you, saying, "Let those who have never sinned be the first to cast stones." They will flash on your face own past weaknesses and imperfections, showing you times when you failed miserably but your spouse graciously spared you a deserved tongue lashing. Moments when you were down and out and your spouse gave you a hug, a kiss, and words of encouragement will become vivid in your mind. But, these entities will only prevail and prove effective to the degree you honor their interventions.

And, before you give up in the face of temporary challenges, these entities will remind you that there is no perfect marriage or perfect partner out there to bring you heavenly bliss. They will encourage you to work harder with the "clay" in your hands and trust God to do the perfect work in your spouse.

Concerning physical, psychological, or emotional challenges that affect sexual performance which is a critical and central dynamic in a marriage relationship, there will be times when your spouse will be willing but unable to deliver the pleasure you once enjoyed in the youthful stages and healthy times (regardless of age) of your married life. For as long as Mary was enjoying good health, our honeymoon was endless. This was one of the strongest dynamic in our marriage relationship and unbelievably, it held true to the very last couple of months before she passed on. She suffered from backache due to gall bladder stones during those last months. (Our relationship was a rare phenomenon because her episodes of depression would force mean long and strenuous periods of sexual abstinence, but in the end, these long breaks enabled me to love and appreciate Mary for herself rather than to view her as a sexual object, only for self-gratification. It helped me develop a brotherly compassion towards Mary. But, whenever my queen was up and running again, we would have a fresh and fiery new beginning to our intimate relationship. It was the honeymoon all over again.) During these tough times of forced abstinence, the entities would urge me to appreciate Mary more, to be patient and not to run, in effect telling me, "Life is not over. The best is yet to come" and sure enough it would come and never fail until death did physically part. That is why my love for Mary and her love for me has gone past the physical separation. Sometimes it feels like Mary is always around somewhere as I often catch myself repeating the words, "I love you my sweet darling" to the pictures on the wall. She also comes alive as I see our children and grandchildren. This book means more to me than to any one else because it immortalizes Mary to me for as long as I live.

In the same way the entities challenged me to be strong during my wife's prolonged periods with depression and kidney disease, they will challenge you through your subconscious and the still small voices deep in your inner recesses. They will ask questions like this: "Suppose you were to exchange positions with your spouse today. How would you like your spouse to treat you, and how would you feel if your spouse abandoned you?" These voices will flood your mind with similar questions, initiating a conversation that will put you on the spot but in the end will inspire you to rise above your circumstances and love your spouse anyhow.

When you contemplate walking away from challenges, the entities will remind you of the divine factor that created your union—the years of sweet and intimate love, the flowers brought to you during occasion, the words of kindness. You will remember all the good deeds, however small, that your spouse has done and the transformations he or she has made happen in you during your marriage. You will recall moments with your little angels, the products of your union, whose birthdays and graduations you have celebrated together over the years with so much pomp and pride as parents and grandparents. These are the same innocent children who gave you a new title: mom or dad, grandma or grandpa and therefore how one careless decision can likely destabilize their future and destiny. Would they be safe on their own without caring parents? Will they have a balanced development under a single parent? Can they be loved by your new partner with no biological link to them? On the other hand, if you failed your children trust in the way you treat their other parent, would they in future be trustworthy to their own spouses? Would you want them to deal with their spouses based on your example? Your children and grandchildren are entities you owe your spouse to.

Have you forgotten the relatives and friends who were there for you from the beginning when you entered into a covenant in their presence and pronounced the words "I do"? Is your decision for a quick exit about to undo those words? Are you rushing to make a permanently harmful decision based on a temporary situation?

Those were some of the subconscious interactions I had with entities I chose to honor and to whom I owed my marriage to Mary. In the toughest moments they came to my aid. In the coming pages I will share in greater detail critical moments in our married life when these entities intervened.

HOW THE ENTITY GOD SPOKE DIRECTLY TO MY SPIRIT

A divine inspiration intervened at my most desperate moment in a matter pertaining to Mary's health. The words "Be faithful; hold on to your Sarah" were dropped into my spirit as if coming directly from the heavenly altar but familiar with the way God speaks to men, I had no doubt that this was God speaking to me. This happened in 1993, soon after depression became clearly evident in my wife, leaving her withdrawn and self-isolated in a room in the home of Mary Ford in Springfield, Virginia, where we lived from 1992 to 1994. These divinely inspired words stuck with me throughout the next twenty-one years of recurring attacks on Mary's health, episodes that always brought great pain and anguish; social, economic, and spiritual disruption to our family but most of all, a freeze to the intimacy in our marriage relationship. The day, the time, and the place these words came remained a vivid memory, becoming a point of reference for strength every time Mary went down with depression and particularly her last five years of life beginning from 2009 when she was diagnosed with terminal kidney disease.

The final and most traumatic test came during her last seven days of life on earth, but the words kept echoing in my spirit, all the same and with the same intensity. All I wanted to do was to remain faithful, steadfastly holding on to my Sarah to the instant of time when she was finally declared unresponsive by the lead doctor in charge of the battery of nurses who relentlessly battled to keep my Mary alive at the Baylor ICU in Irving, Texas. The doctor came to the waiting room where Caroline, Armstrong, and I were huddled and asked if I as the husband could make the hardest decision of my life. She asked whether I wanted the battle for Mary's life to continue, whether they should still try to resuscitate her as she kept falling back into a coma every time they thought they had succeeded. The doctor told us how precarious the situation had become because Mary's rib cage was caving in from the physical pressure, and blood transfusions were coming right out through every orifice of her body. That was the last thing I wanted to hear happening to the woman I idolized for forty years of my life and willing to die for any time. I felt so helpless and extremely emotionally distraught but I held up for the sake of my children. I found myself again like in times past, in a situation, "you are dumb if you do it, you are dumb if you don't." It was truly a dilemma for me. But I decided to let my children weigh in more on this most strenuous decision presented to us. I asked the doctor for a family moment.

The decision facing me as the final decision maker was gigantic. I kept wondering quietly whether that moment had finally come when I should let Sarah go to her maker. This was the Sarah I was instructed long ago to hold onto and never contemplated giving up on her even at the most desperate moment, times when she laid in a bed, for days and nights due to depression, refusing to eat or go to hospital, days turning into months and then into a year. She would not talk to me or even to other members of our family. Yet, even in those moments I never gave up on her, abandon her or leave her on her own but instead, I had her hospitalized and treated involuntarily because I considered myself as owing her to God and to Mary herself on her own merits for the innumerable benefits she had brought to my life. I owed her to our relatives and friends, and most of all to my two young children, who were now standing next to me as adults with their own families. I had won their trust over the years in the way I cared for their mother.

I turned to Caroline, my firstborn and my best counsel, for her opinion. She shared with us her final conversation with the mother, when she told Caroline that she was tired and wanted to rest and then to my son Armstrong who felt strongly that his mother had bravely fought her battle long enough and it was her time to rest. In response, and with a clear conscience, I summed up our joint position: thus far, we had gallantly fought a good fight, we had kept the faith and having done all we could do, it was time to stand as one and let God give His servant the well-deserved rest. As for me, It was time to hand over Sarah to the one who spoke to me twenty-one years earlier, saying, "Be faithful; hold onto your Sarah." It was hard for each of us but momentarily, sadness was lifted and our hearts were at peace, we then send for the doctor to give her the green light to let Mary rest in peace because we were at peace, fully showered in the love she had shown to each of us to the last day and also to know that we all loved her dearly. Mary passed on peacefully. Amazingly, after she was cleaned up and dressed, we (Myself, Caroline, Armstrong and Jerusha Nkoyo) went back into her room when her body was still warm and soft to our touch, taking picture around her and recalling her humor as she laid there beautiful as ever, with peace, love, joy and faith shining through her lifeless body. The same phenomenon was repeated about two weeks later at the funeral home. It was one day before her funeral when we went to view her embalmed body dressed in her ministerial regalia. We were all there: myself, Caroline, Waithaka, Armstrong and Jerusha (his wife). This was another moment of joy as we witnessed the same glorious image of a woman who lived all her live sharing love with her family and friends and serving God who called her from the days of her youth.

"BE FAITHFUL; HOLD ON TO YOUR SARAH"

God's message saying, "Be faithful; hold on to your Sarah," came at a time when my family of four was living with a fine Christian widow, Mary Ford, who by divine provision opened her five-bedroom home in Springfield, Virginia, to us in September 1992 (As detailed in later pages, my wife miraculously led us to this home where our room and board were completely provided for two solid years to the time we were on our own with a status allowing us to get jobs and rent our own apartment in Alexandria Virginia). This unique "manna" from above started flowing just two months after our arrival from Kenya, but it was a continuation of God's divine providence of what had begun from day one at Brother Paul Adam's home in Massachusetts for two weeks before arriving at the Calvary Pentecostal Tabernacle in Ashland Virginia where our room and board was 100 percent covered (all these were benefits from Mary's God-ordered footsteps. She had led the way to USA five months earlier). But, notably coming from Kenya, we had no definite plan on where to start our journey in America after Calvary Pentecostal Camp ended, and neither were we materially prepared for the unforeseen health challenges which Mary was to encounter. But the divine entity, God, was sufficient for all our needs to overflow because, God had us adopted by a well to do and loving white widow lady who became a mother to us and a grandmother to our children yet without any prior historical or racial link.

During those two years, we never knew what it cost to live as comfortably in America as we found ourselves suddenly living. Our comfort surpassed what we had enjoyed as diplomats in Washington, D.C., ten years earlier (1982–84) when all that was provided was housing and we had to buy our own groceries but at Mary Ford's home, providence was 100%. We soon became the envy of our friends, who discovered how large we were living when they came to see us. We ate and drank for free in a spacious home in an affluent neighborhood as the adopted family of Mary Ford. Her children were grown and off living with their families. We called her "Mama Ford" and our children called her "grandma." Mary Ford, seventy-two years old when we arrived, considered herself privileged to serve God by ministering to us. She even did our laundry like any mother and grandmother and at times cooked and baked for us.

While we were staying at this home, my wife experienced early menopause. She was thirty-seven years old. According to experts, this occurred at too early an age, which more often than not leads to depression. For Mary the premature transition indeed triggered depression, and by September 1993 it was full blown. She dropped out of the Bible College where we were theology students. She moved out of our assigned bedroom at the home and barricaded herself in an extra vacant room where she would sleep all day and all night, sneaking out in the middle of the night to make herself a cup of tea and to have a slice or two of buttered bread after everybody else had retired to bed. She would then return to bed. None of us had access to her at any time of day or night.

The buttered bread was Mary's lone meal each day, and the walk from her room to the kitchen and the bathroom was her only physical activity and only when nobody could see her. For several months, that was her routine. As a result, she fell to almost half her normal weight. Her skin turned pale due to a lack of sunlight and to an unhealthy diet although there was plenty of food and sunshine available. She would not talk to any of us in the home, anyone in America or call Kenya.

Confused and shocked, I asked myself many questions without answers, the main one being why my adored wife and best friend of fourteen years at the time had suddenly withdrawn, turning her back on the man she adoringly loved from high school days, her two children, who meant the world to her or even our host who had shown such unsurpassed generosity. I kept wondering whether a rebellious spirit had taken hold of her during the five months she had been alone in America. But I recalled how excited she had been for months after we first arrived and how she had led us to Mary Ford's home, and prophetically declaring that this was the place God would have us to stay until we could move into a home of our own (a prophecy that held true perpetually and literally ended with a place of our own two years later). Judging by her character and history, I was sure there could not be another man in her life because she was not having conversations or visiting with anyone, but the mystery of Mary's disconnect deepened as I found no logical explanation for her "strange" behavior as I saw it. Unfortunately, I had no prior knowledge or understanding of depression and how the ailment manifests.

We prayed hard with the children and with our host. I fasted for a divine answer and for a clear direction on what I needed to do about an unfamiliar situation at the beginning of my journey in America. I kept wondering what could have happened had the problem begun at the camp meeting campus of Calvary Pentecostal Tabernacle in Ashland, Virginia, where our journey began and worst still, had this situation arisen if we were on our own renting an apartment and depending on a combined income to support ourselves. But thank God, for he had foreseen all that and prepared a shelter for us at Mary Ford's home way ahead.

All these thoughts were going through my mind when one morning, while I was in our assigned bedroom, God spoke to me by dropping into my spirit the words, "Be faithful; hold on to your Sarah." These words were accompanied by Scripture. Twenty-one years later, the words and the prevailing circumstances at the time remain vivid. The message came on Thursday, September 2, 1993; I noted the date on the Bible page I was reading, next to 2 Samuel 22:2–7. The event took place as I was getting ready for my morning devotions.

The meaning of the words was not immediately clear, because I was not Abraham, my wife was not Sarah, and they did not fit the context of the accompanying Scripture. However, as time went by and I studied Abraham, it dawned on me that obedience and faithfulness were the hallmarks of his character. Still, these traits had to be tested and found to hold true. In the end, Abraham remained faithful and content with a barren woman, and for all the years they were married, Abraham never took an interest in another woman until Sarah herself proposed that he get a child through her maid. "And Sarai Abram's wife took Hagar her maid the Egyptian, after Abram had dwelt ten years in the land of Canaan, and gave her to her husband Abram to be his wife" (Genesis 16:3 KJV).

In this and many other ways, Abraham won God's favor through faithfulness, and so God opened Sarah's womb to conceive Isaac, the son of promise, at advanced ages for both of them. "For Sarah conceived, and bare Abraham a son in his old age, at the set time of which God had spoken to him" (Genesis 21:2 KJV). Abraham's faith is also referenced in the New

Testament: "He staggered not at the promise of God through unbelief; but was strong in faith, giving glory to God" (Romans 4:20 KJV). As long as I remained faithful and did not abandon Mary during her health tribulations, the promises of Abraham would apply to me for the rest of my life with her and beyond both of us just as Abraham and his seed prospered because he had been obedient, holding on to the mother of promise to the end. All that was required of me was to faithfully hold on to my Mary, a minister of the gospel and the mother of my seed.

These Scripture passages laid a firm foundation for dealing with all the health challenges that I would face through my Sarah in the next twenty years. And throughout her years of on-and-off hospitalization, Mary's health expenses (for depression and kidney disease treatment and for medical tests by a host of specialists) were supernaturally covered to the tune of hundreds of thousands of dollars. Her funeral expenses (including my prepaid spot by her side) at Blue Bonnet Hills family Park and Cemetery in Colleyville Texas, one of the best cemeteries in the United States were also paid off through divine providence. All I needed to do was to faithfully offer moral, physical, and spiritual support to Mary.

The God to whom I owed Mary gave me the Scriptures at my hour of greatest need, and during the twenty-one-year journey, He provided all the resources necessary to care for her. During the last stages of her kidney disease, Mary was placed in the disability category of patients, enabling her to access benefits including a monthly check, which she used mostly to do the work of her International Prayer Network ministry. Her benefits also included a tax exemption that applied to our homestead.

Intervention by the divine entity, God, brought a message that became the foundation of my faithfulness and helped me hold on to my covenant with Mary throughout an often-turbulent journey. And in the final phase, lasting five years, when the turbulence rose a notch higher, God raised the standard and through His abundance, supplied all of our spiritual, physical, emotional, and material needs in the same way He had provided for us when we were hosted by Mary Ford. This was in line with Scripture, which says, " Now unto him that is able to do exceeding abundantly above all that we ask or think, according to the power that worketh in us" (Ephesians 3:20 KJV).

Lessons from Mary's initial crisis prepared us for future troubles and as a family, we knew exactly what we had to do and were sure we could count on God's abundant providence every time Mary commenced a downward spiral as a result of secret withdrawal from her antidepressants. The cycle brought a time of great anxiety to us as her family. Mary would be withdrawn and become uncooperative with any suggestion to go to hospital, denying she was sick and would get angry (even though non-verbal) at any suggestion that she was sick. Her diet would suffer and she would become uncommunicative. She would then develop life-threatening physical weakness due to malnutrition. The longest episode lasted for more than a year—from withdrawal to involuntary hospitalization. Involuntary hospitalization and a restart of antidepressants would follow (in Mary's case, this phase might take two to six weeks). Thereafter, she would need six months to a year to fully regain her physical strength and self-confidence. For Mary, the whole cycle would last close to two years, followed by about three years total freedom from depression with compliance in taking antidepressants before the next episode after secret withdrawal as a result of over confidence and belief that she was finally healed and needed no antidepressants. This is a common characteristic with many who suffer from depression.

To get her into involuntary commitment and treatment program, we used the life-threatening state (due to malnutrition) as evidence to satisfy the law requirements. I had to go through a judicial process each time Mary went down with depression, but after two or three weeks of treatment she was clear of her foggy mindedness and on her way to full physical recovery. Soon after recovery this model wife and mother who would resume her central role in the family, take up jobs, and do ministry work as if nothing ever happened.

In March 2001 we decided to relocate from Virginia to accept a job offer as home parents at a highly reputable children's home in Waco, Texas. This was an ideal opportunity since we longed to move closer to Baylor University where Caroline had been admitted as an undergraduate in 1999. She was still too young and we wanted to be nearby. But soon after we moved and started the job, Mary, as in the past, became overconfident about her wellness, a common phenomenon with people suffering from depression. She would often forget to take her daily antidepressant pill as we got busy with the hustle and bustle of youth care.

At some point, Mary finally decided to quit the medication altogether, and before long she started losing the drive and interest in the job. These tell-tale signs were common in the early stages of past depression episodes. She was soon deep into stage one of the cycle and could not continue with the job, quitting around June 2001and sleeping 24/7 at home. That affected my service as a Home Parent and had to move to another department of the Youth Care Program because we could serve only as a couple. Mary had to go through the whole cycle and wasn't ready to return to Home Parenting work again until February 2005. The home considered us a model couple and that was the only reason we returned to home parenting. Mary performed way beyond expectations as we worked together taking care of dysfunctional youths for the next three years in total at that home and another Children Home in Round Rock Texas. Then we decided to take a break so we could enter the mission field. Part of the work involved a one-month visit to Kenya in June 2008.

The entity God became my greatest ally—a source of hope, of physical and emotional strength, and of all the material resources needed to deal with Mary's health issues. Whether she was flying high at her best moments or crawling on her belly at her weakest points, God showed His faithfulness and providence by intervening in our lives. And when Mary passed, God supplied every need toward her funeral expenses.

When the words "Be faithful; hold on to your Sarah" came to me by inspiration of the Holy Spirit. I was at the bottom of a valley of despair and uncertainty because of Mary's condition. We were College students hosted by Mary Ford in her home. I had no job and no health insurance, and so Mary's condition caused me great anxiety. But God, who had faithfully supplied us with His manna through Mary Ford, had a plan to cover my wife's treatment for twenty-one years and to take care of her funeral expenses. All that God wanted me to do throughout that period was "Be faithful; hold on to your Sarah," and I obeyed. As time passed, the Scripture verses that accompanied these words became more alive until the day we laid Mary to rest. To quote:

> And he said, The Lord is my rock, and my fortress, and
> my deliverer; the God of my rock; in him will I trust: he
> is my shield, and the horn of my salvation, my high tower,

and my refuge, my saviour; thou savest me from violence. I will call on the Lord, who is worthy to be praised: so shall I be saved from mine enemies. When the waves of death compassed me, the floods of ungodly men made me afraid; the sorrows of hell compassed me about; the snares of death prevented me; in my distress I called upon the Lord, and cried to my God: and he did hear my voice out of his temple, and my cry did enter into his ears. (2 Samuel 22:2-7 KJV)

In essence, God's message to hold onto my Sarah made me His debtor. I had to take care of His valued child and servant of the gospel. He knew that this would be a treacherous journey and that I would need His supernatural power to climb the hills and to descend the deep valleys, sometimes with Mary on my back (something that became a reality at different occasions). I still remember one morning in Waco Texas when I came home from work to find Mary almost unconscious. Her blood sugar had dropped dangerously low overnight. But instead of calling 911, a practice that is automatic in America, I quickly dressed her, put her on my back, and raced down two flights of stairs to the ground floor of our mansion in Waco Texas and out of the door. I placed her in the back seat of our car and frantically rushed her to emergency room in Providence Hospital.

In retrospect, my "crazy" love for Mary and the blind belief that only I could handle her with care she deserved and keep her from harm must have clouded my reasoning that morning. This is a reminder of the story shared by Mrs. Mary Gathunguri at the beginning of this book where after Mary went missing from my home town, I took my soldiers with me from Gilgil barracks and went looking for her in Nairobi city just in case she was there and in danger. God knew of my obsession with Mary and gave me supernatural strength both physical and emotional as seen in the case when my family was attacked by thugs at night in Limuru town. The thought alone that Mary could be vulnerable inspired a supernatural courage and strength in me to resist the attackers for several hours (story in coming chapter)

I owed Mary to God and whenever I needed special strength to take care and protect her, He gave it to me. Do you owe your spouse to your God? Are you His faithful steward?

MARY AS AN ENTITY

My second source of inspiration and motivation in those difficult years came from Mary herself through the stories she had shared with me soon after we joined her in the United States. She recounted what she had endured and how she had fasted and prayed for miracles for her daily provisions and for doors to open for me and the children to join her. That was her daily prayer during the five months she had been in United States alone, looking for ways to bring us over. She recalled how she met Mary Ford, who would eventually adopt our family for two years, providing everything we needed to be as comfortable as any other middle-class family in America, though we had no past relationship with her.

These stories of daring faith, courage, and self-sacrifice kept replaying in my mind as Mary had narrated them in her sweet voice before she went down with depression. They were a reminder of many previous heroic moments when Mary's faith and courage had saved our lives. As she lay isolated in that room, covered head to toe under sheets and blankets and saying absolutely nothing to me, the more loudly her voice would replay inside me, repeating the stories of trials and triumphs. That mysterious inner voice led me to realize more than ever how important Mary was to me and how deeply I was indebted to her. I owed Mary to Mary's own merits. She had earned my love, admiration, and favor above anyone else I had encountered in my adult life, and that belief remained a cornerstone for the rest of our life together. Are you a debtor to your spouse? Does this make your spouse invaluable to you? Does that sense of indebtedness enhance purpose in your marriage?

OUR CHILDREN AS AN ENTITY

The innocent faces of my worried and traumatized children became another entity that motivated me never to give up on their mother.

Armstrong (eleven) and Caroline (thirteen) must have been very concerned about how their mother's health would affect our future as a family and in particular their parents' relationship. They had never experienced this kind of coldness by their mother towards their father before this time, instead, their parents were obsessed with each other from as far back as they could remember, always addressing each other as "my beloved." They never fought or scream at each other but strangely, their mother was now not communicating to him or to them at all. That must have frightened and devastated them, especially the older Caroline, but they did not verbalize their feelings.

I was acutely aware of their fears and uncertainty. They needed constant reassurance in word and deed that I would never abandon them or the mother they adored. They knew of husbands who abandoned their wives and their children and had gone on to new lives with other women, and they had reasons to be worried. But the children did not know our story going back to the time we met as teenagers in high school—how obsessed we were with each other, how strong and deep the love chemistry between us had been, and how that was multiplied after we got married and had them as our children. They had no idea how strongly their birth had cemented our commitment to each other and the degree to which I considered myself a debtor to them as far as owing them a mother was concerned and therefore how far I would go to ensure that they would always have a mother, a woman secure in my love whether or not she was talking to me.

I grew up around a mother who was always sickly. As far as I could remember, going back to 1959 (when I was only five years old) to 1991 when she passed, my mother had always health issues and yet my father, who was not a born again Christian never abandoned her. Nothing meant more to me that coming home from school to find my mother home waiting to receive me with a dish she had made in spite of her poor health. On the day I got married (1979) my lovely mother and my father, my two heroes, were there as seen in the picture section of this book. My father remarried soon after my mother passed, he was around sixty eight years old. Today, my father in his early 90's is my best friend and so is his young wife. This friendship and respect is not just about his being my biological father, but stems from the way he loved and treated my mother when she needed him and I needed her most. While he had opportunities to move on with another healthy woman and abandon my mother, he chose not to because he understood what a mother meant to a child. For more than thirty years, my father stuck with my sickly mother thus giving me a gift I could never repay, a mother who lived a full life (about sixty five) and lived to see and babysit my own children as their grandmother.

I had a role model, my own father set an example for me and now it was my turn to imitate that for my children. I considered this an entitlement for my children. I owed a mother to them in sickness or in health. Do you owe your spouse to your children? Are you their faithful steward? Does this add to your purpose in marriage?

Consideration of our relatives and friends from both sides

During my tribulations over Mary's depression, I heard from relatives on both sides of the family, though they were thirteen thousand miles away, then from friends scattered across the world, and finally from our closest Christians brethren, who had come to know of my plight. Some called to tell me that they were praying for us and counting on me as their son, brother, and friend to stand strong for my sick and disconnected wife, whom they had known, loved and trusted for years and who was dear to them as a daughter, sister, and friend. All these entities, whom I respected, honored, and owed a great deal, had one message throughout our crisis: "Wilfred, never give up on our daughter, sister, and friend. She is too precious to all of us." They encouraged me to fight and not to flee as many did when faced with similar situations.

Their images occupied my thoughts, persuading me to stay focused and not to yield to temptation and seek comfort outside of marriage rather than in God. With this encouragement, I was fortified and ready to fight like a man who trusted God, the husband of a great woman who had endeared herself to a multitude of loving relatives and caring friends and whose dignity had ennobled me. I resolved to do whatever it took to protect the interests of relatives and friends invested in Mary, I was the steward to whom they had entrusted her care. Do you owe your spouse to your relatives and friends? Are you their steward? Does this add purpose to your marriage?

Whether in sickness or in health, in joy or in sadness, I loved and treasured my wife because I owed her first and foremost to God, who gave her to me; to Mary's own innumerable merits; to our children, who deserved a loved and secure mother; to our relatives, to our closest family friends, and to the entire household of faith. My sense of indebtedness to all these entities became my strongest anchor.

A purpose-driven marriage can be born only out of a sense of owing your spouse to entities beyond yourself, including that spouse. These are entities you respect and choose to honour with your marriage union. With such a marriage no mountain is too high to climb and no valley too deep to be crossed.

To whom do you owe your spouse? To whom will you turn to gain the purpose to persist when the going gets tough?

THE VALUE SYSTEMS THAT SHAPED OUR WORLD VIEWS

Mary Muthoni Mbuthuri had one advantage in her upbringing: her parents were early converts to the Salvation Army faith in East Africa. Her father, Dishon Mbuthuri, rose to the rank of brigadier in the Salvation Army, and his supportive wife, Dorcas Wangari Mbuthuri, rose with him. Dishon Mbuthuri established the foundation for most of the Salvation Army ministries and projects in Kenya. He headed the organization's first officer cadet training institution. As a missionary family, the Mbuthuris traveled throughout the country, planting churches and initiating charitable projects. Their ministry spanned more than fifty years.

Mary, the fifth born in her family, grew up in an environment saturated with religion and great values. Her parents were faithful, of high moral standards, forthright, and honest in their religious practices and had a positive influence on their children and grandchildren. They prayed and believed in divine providence for food, clothing, school fees, and shelter.

I had the unique privilege of knowing Mary's parents. Her mother died in 1976, only two years after Mary and I met in high school. She was generous and friendly and welcomed me into the family as soon as she realized that her daughter and I were serious friends and that we attended the same school. She treated me like one of her own children and never worried for daughter when Mary visited my home in Narok almost two hundred miles away. Though she never got to meet my parents, she trusted that the family story her daughter and I told her was genuine. Mary's mother loved and respected me like one of her sons and introduced me to her friends that way, adding to my bond with Mary. She had passed on when we tied the knot in 1979, but the love, trust, and faith she showed for me bore fruit throughout our marriage. I was deeply indebted to her, and the only way I could pay that debt was to love, respect, honor, trust, and protect Mary with God's help.

Over the years, whenever Mary fell into depression and could not communicate with me for months on end, I used to pass by her bed and uncover her face slightly to say hello and to express my love for her. To my surprise, I would see the image of her beautiful mother, whom she very much resembled, before she quickly pulled back the cover. That image would bring back many affectionate memories of a person I had come to love and honor and to whom I was so much indebted for letting me love her daughter. Mary's mother seemed to be telling me, "This is my beloved daughter, the girl I entrusted to you before you married her. Please love her and take care of her for me."

Everything about my relationship with Mary's mother applies to my relationship with her father, a gracious man. He was on hand on October 13, 1979, to give his beloved daughter to me (as seen in the pictures section). Throughout the years of our courtship and after our marriage to the time he died, he was always fatherly to me and a best friend. I was indebted to him when he was alive, and after he died, I wanted to love and honor Mary for him.

Mary's parents lived out their faith daily, and their marriage was a model for their children. Christian faith as taught in Scripture became their family culture, their nature, and their system of values! That is what Mary inherited. The God of her parents became her God; their perspectives on life became her perspectives.

In 1973, Mary changed from her parents' religion, the Salvation Army, to become a Pentecostal charismatic, this move only helped to reinforce the values she had inherited from them. She had been taught to fear God and to put Him first. Mary brought all these superior values to our marriage.

A CONTRAST OF VALUES IN OUR BACKGROUNDS

My parents, Onesimus Mwaura Nkoyo and Leah Wanjiku Nkoyo, had nine children, five boys and four girls. I was third-born of those alive and second-born of the boys. We inherited the Kikuyu traditions, my parents' roots by birth, and the Maasai traditions, where my parents were adopted before we were born. Our parents brought us up with these mixed cultural values, which centered on honesty, hard work, hospitality, and generosity. But by the early '40s, my parents' values had been greatly influenced by Christian missionaries sponsored by African Inland Missions (AIM), who reached out into our Maasai district, operating from their mission center (a school and a hospital) established in 1901 at Kijabe on the slopes of the Great Rift Valley in Kenya.

These missionaries spread the gospel into the interior, reaching the Narok region in the early '40s and building churches, schools, and medical clinics. My parents embraced the basic AIM Christian doctrine. They learned to pray and to recite a few Scripture verses, but because they lacked formal education and attended church irregularly, by the time I was a teenager they had lost most of what they had learned. The values I got from my parents were therefore a mixture of Christianity and customary beliefs.

My conversion came without input from my parents. I began a brand-new lifestyle in 1970 after my conversion at sixteen through the Pentecostal Assemblies of God Church and left behind my parents' traditional beliefs as I fully embraced Christianity (see my pictures after conversion in the pictures section). The values of respect for adults and obedience they taught me were reinforced and better defined by the biblical teaching of my newfound faith.

My father initially took a wait-and-see attitude toward my conversion. He thought that I would soon give up Christianity. He saw this conversion as a betrayal of tradition, which he believed gave me identity including my name. This may explain why Christianity had not taken root in my parents. They had been brought up to view Christianity as a white man's religion, designed to counter their cultural beliefs and values, but this attitude never deterred me from growing in the faith. I had an advantage they did not have: the ability to read the Bible for myself and constant involvement with church folks, especially a new generation of missionaries who were quite aggressive in reaching the young through academic institutions that they staffed while evangelizing among students. These gave birth to indigenous youth groups reaching out to young people in schools and colleges.

My father soon discovered that my new faith had greatly improved on the values he taught me, especially concerning obedience, respect for adults, and trustworthiness. I became more focused in school, and my exemplary performance gave my parents much pride. That led to his conviction and conversion in December of 1974 during one of the most memorable three-day crusades that my high school sweetheart Mary and I as teenagers organized during our Christmas school break and preached in Narok's open market.

My father's main challenge came from years of watching me grow into something better than he had envisioned for me. Christianity had given me a new tradition, a positive network of friends—especially sweet Mary, my fiancée—and a new set of values, which were far superior to my cultural values. My father, my older sister Beth, and an uncle got converted to Christ during those crusades and became active in church. Soon after, my mother and my brother joined them, and they were all baptized into the faith in my church denomination. Forty years later, my father who is ninety one this year, is still a staunch believer and a sponsor of a church he built on land he donated. My mother and sister died still confessing their faith in Jesus Christ, and my older brother remains a born-again Christian.

THE MILITARY VALUES SYSTEM AND THE MARY FACTOR

By the time I joined the army in 1976, I was a mature Christian. Initially it was hard to reconcile the military way of doing things with my new nature as a Christian. Whereas I had become used to persuading and motivating others to do things, the officer's rank for which I was being trained demanded I order others under my command to obey without question. I was expected to do the same when my superiors ordered me, and I had to learn the hard way. I got a rude shock when for the first time as an officer cadet in 1976 I was instructed to conduct an ammunition clearance inspection on a firing range. This is a routine practice at the end of every firing exercise to ensure that no participant forgets a live bullet in the barrel or the chamber of a gun, in the pocket, or the pouches.

I was supposed to march to the front of my squad, already in a single file, shout specific words of command, and walk along the formation, inspecting each individual. I was then supposed to march to where the officer in charge of the firing range was standing and declare to him that all was clear in my squad. As I marched to the front, the first word that came out of my mouth was *please* followed by others that I can't remember since I was cut short by the fire-breathing noncommissioned officer and rudely ordered to raise my rifle and run around the field as a punishment for using a term that doesn't exist in any military command manual. At the end, I was told to forget the word *please* for as long as I was in the military because it was not part of military language. I found that to be true from the time I served in combat troops until I went for staff training and was posted to serve as a military diplomat in Washington, D.C. That was years later, from 1982 to 1984.

The military was not on my list of career choices at the beginning, but a colleague who taught in a secondary school with me and a mentor from my home church persuaded me to change my mind. My colleague begged me to accompany him to a recruitment day. He had tried unsuccessfully several times to join the military. I consulted with my spiritual mentor at church on whether joining the military would conflict with my Christian faith. He highly recommended that I go for the interviews and offered to pray for me. Mary's brother-in-law, Dr. Wilson Waciira, a captain and a doctor for the recruiting team, also encouraged me to try.

Only two people had to be kept completely in the dark on this plan: Mary, my fiancée, who was in her last year in the advanced level at Nyandarua High School, and my mother, who after learning that I had begun military training, fasted for two weeks in an effort to extricate me from the system. But Mary who could not be in the dark forever soon discovered where her sweetheart was and became a frequent visitor to see me at the college. In the end, I graduated from military training college in

April 1977 among the top three honor officer cadets out of fifty. I received an award from Kenya's president and commander in chief. I was then posted to the Kenya army artillery corps in Gilgil.

Here, my life started taking a soldierly turn: my thinking and my world view were fast tending to the military value system at the expense of the Christian concept (apart from my moral views). That trend would change after Mary came into my life with our marriage in 1979. She reconciled my military and Christian values, establishing a balance that made me whole. She reordered my life: a Christian first, a husband and an army officer. That became my way of life and what I was known for during the rest of my time in the service. But even then, I still struggled with issues of "works and faith."

During my officer training, I had been reprimanded for using the word *please*, and that indoctrination exercise sank deep into my subconscious mind. With time, military discipline had a huge impact on my Christian practices. Christianity teaches that all things are possible for those who believe. The military's view is that all things are possible for those who work hard. During training, the message is that all things are possible with the army. More often than not, the soldier in me rather than my Christian faith came to the fore. "The soldier in me had to make things work and nothing is impossible to him" this was the case and attitude during active service and after retirement. Before calling out to heaven for answers, I would turn to the arm of flesh for solutions. I worked hard trying to make things happen rather than waiting for answers after praying. The military doctrine positively affected my Christian faith in one respect, making me fearless in action, On the other hand, it had a negative impact: overreliance on the flesh.

Mary worked on me in this area throughout our marriage. She had the patience I could not muster. We would pray for things or about family issues, and Mary would sleep soundly, assured of the miraculous but I would find myself wide awake, turning in bed or pacing the floor, trying to figure out some solution. Mary would wake up, disrupted by my movement, and she would wonder why I was still awake. I would explain that I couldn't sleep until I knew what to do about the problem. She would ask me, "Didn't we pray about it?" I would hoarsely retort, "Yes, I know we did, but we still have to figure out some solution." She would go back to sleep, asking me, "What was the purpose of praying if you are still working for your solution instead of waiting for God's?" But the soldier in me would reply, "Soldiers pray on their feet to the place of action and always with their eyes open to keep track of enemy movement," arguing that we had to fight for our miracle and stay alert to what the enemy was doing. After all, Scripture teaches that faith without works is dead and that we must watch and pray (James 2:20 and Mathew 26:41 NKJV). That used to be my counter argument to Mary.

But as time passed, I realized that my military machismo doctrine, "All things are possible with the army," was limited to certain physical situations, and even then, we needed divine intervention. For example, in 1990, we were attacked at night and the soldier in me instinctively sprang into combat even though I was unarmed, I knew I had to stand up and fight and not run or let the enemy overrun me. No one could come near my Mary or my children without a fight to the end. But God supernaturally intervened, enabling me to repulse a multitude that had demolished twenty-one windows and eight doors and had pulled down part of the roof of our house. In this instance and others that I will share, Mary's foundational doctrine of faith and weapon of war—summed up in one short verse, "I can do all things through Christ which strengtheneth me" (Philippians 4:13 KJV)—was always a superior weapon, far mightier than the mightiest army or the tough soldier in me.

MARY'S DOMESTICATION OF WILFRED AND DEMILITARIZATION OF THE NKOYO HOME

I can find no better words than *domestication* and *demilitarization* to describe Mary's influence on my attitude and in shaping our home and family life. The first breakfast that Mary served me in our home after our honeymoon included an egg omelet, but she made it very differently from the way the cook prepared it at the officers club (mess) where I ate all my meals in my years as a single officer. Our head cook, Mr. Kofa, had special training in five-star hotel catering, and our quarters were cleaned and maintained by assigned enlisted men with the title Batman, one to each officer. Their duties included doing laundry, shinning officer's boots and ceremonial attire, and caring for an officer's battle kit and tent in the field. In my day, officers were really spoilt. We had real and unique privileges (may be because there were fewer commissioned officers compared to present) and that's why when Mary went missing, I could afford to take my military jeep and my soldiers with enough ration to last a whole weekend of "search and rescue." I could also call my hometown police station and demand that whoever was suspect or culpable in this disappearance be picked up and locked up until they can tell what they knew about Mary, a wife of a Kenya army officer in Gilgil (military officers were highly esteemed in civil circles in my days).

That pride and excessive privileges are a baggage I unconsciously tried to sneak into my married life, to the point I wanted my Batman to come often into our home and take care of my kit but Mary nipped this trend in the bud, learning to do most of these things herself so she could take over.

At that first breakfast a new life began for me. On that morning, I realized that I had to forget what was behind and focus on what was ahead. My adorable queen had sneaked out early from our bedroom to make her king a maiden breakfast. She then tiptoed back, bearing the steaming hot breakfast, and placed it carefully on the bedside table. She intended to surprise the man who meant the world to her with this labor of love.

But this man needed work, and that would be Mary's first test. She did not tap on my forehead or call me "my beloved," as she usually did. This time she planted a hot kiss on my lips. As I opened my eyes, I was for a moment mesmerized by the angelic look on my adored bride's face. The light coming through the windows gave her a special glow that made me think I was in some heavenly realm in the company of angels, an impression enhanced by her special multicolored nightgown, among the gifts I had brought her from Pakistan (where I had been sent for artillery training just before we got married).

Mary wanted to surprise me with the artistry of her cooking, but when I came to, the sight of the egg omelet immediately put me off. I was insensitive to the intensity of the passion surrounding that first meal and the meaning of the moment to her, and still under the strong influence of the military single life and cook Kofa's stylish catering, I made a terrible blunder. I said, "Thanks, love, for this omelet, but it doesn't look quite like what Kofa makes at the officers mess." I paid a price and learned a lesson I would not forget for the rest of our life together. This became a turning point. I discovered the meanings of the words *domestication* and *demilitarization* and found out that Mary was fully in charge of these two critical programs of Wilfred transformation.

Though Mary had visited me a couple of times at the officers mess during our courtship, she had little knowledge of my cushy officer's life and had not visited my quarters (on grounds of our Christian values). She had no idea who Kofa was and knew nothing about his cooking or his qualifications, but none of that information mattered to Mary. Wilfred had to be domesticated and to learn that he was no longer a bachelor in the single officers' quarters, dining in an officers mess from Kofa's dishes, but at home from Mary's dishes and that this family home was a demilitarized zone even though it was physically located within the military barracks. His family space was a retreat different from the rigid military life. "Okay, my love," Mary said very softly and continued, "Kofa will no longer make you the omelet. I will for the rest of your life, but I want you to know this: it is not just about an omelet but all your meals and drinks henceforth, which will come in a special wrapping, my love and admiration for you, every moment and always." An elegant woman of few words, spoken with love and utmost respect to the man she would lovingly serve every day and every moment for the next thirty five years concluded.

With those words, the matter was settled for the next thirty-five years. I would eat and drink from Mary's dining table, not only from her choice plates and silverware, but from her lovely hands many times. Once in a while, I would be spoiled with a treat placed in my mouth with her beautiful fingers and we would drink from one cup. Kofa and his top-notch cooking became history, and I never had a desire to visit the club again either for his meals or to hang out with my buddies, because a day of Mary's companionship and love exceeded the pleasure derived from a year at officer's mess with the best of my friends. After all, I did not drink any wine or alcohol at any time in my life. Our children, our families, and our friends always commented about Mary's great cooking, and I enjoyed it until the day Mary made her last meal for me before leaving this life. I am forever indebted to this woman whose boldness and love domesticated me. She also taught me to cook, something I take pride in doing for my children and grandchildren in their homes and in our home whenever they visit.

Mary took a different approach to demilitarization. Her dream was to open our home for Bible study and fellowship to all in her new military family. Initially, since I was a commissioned officer living in exclusive officer mansions and exclusively officers section of the barracks, the attendees would be limited to officers and their wives. But Mary's passion for souls went beyond the bounds of segregation by rank. She began by inviting the wives of officers and enlisted men for ladies' fellowship at our home. This birthed one of the most powerful military wives' fellowships of our times at the Kenyatta barracks in Gilgil. The wives' influence led most of their husbands to convert, and soon our home became a meeting place for Military Christian Fellowship, which gathered once a week.

Mary looked forward to these nights; she made sure to provide tea and buns for consumption as an extended fellowship after the main Bible study. The members, especially the enlisted men, also looked forward to the night, just to be at an environment where they could freely mingle with officers addressing each other as brother and sister. They nicknamed Mary "Mama Kanisa," Kiswahili words for "church mother" or "mother of church." Through this fellowship, Mary managed to create a rank-free environment where there was no regard for rank and was open to all. Christ was the Commander-In-Chief at Mary's home.

But Mary went a step further. She knew that military barracks and camps were off limits to civilians, but she considered her family residence exempt from that rule. From time to time, she invited outsiders for fellowship to our home. Mary would boldly pull up to the strictly controlled barracks gates with brethren in our unique red Mercedes-Benz any time of the day or night. Most of the guards knew the car, the driver, and where she was heading. They would approach the car, look inside, and silently note her passengers. Then they would greet Mama Kanisa and ask whether this was the fellowship night. If it was, she would say yes and extend an invitation. The guards would ask whether those were her Christian guests. She would say yes, and that was enough. The process was always short and ended with the words, "God bless you, Mama Kanisa."

Bringing guests into the camp without scrutiny was a privilege nobody else, including me or the camp commandant, enjoyed. But Mary, a civilian had earned trust from the servicemen who watched the gate. That was how she managed the demilitarization project during our twelve years of military service. Mary was inducted into the military family in style through marriage and discovered a rich mission field and a wonderful community inside the barracks. Using her privileged access and freedoms she applied herself aggressively and boldly, bearing fruit that outlasted her access and eventually her earthly life. Even now, there is still a huge remnant of that fruit inside the Kenyatta barracks and the surrounding area in Gilgil because Mary's faith dared to go where even angels feared to tread: past military traditions, restrictions, and segregation by rank to bring the light of the gospel.

During the most difficult times, Mary was always the first ally I would call. She had become a pillar of strength and the calm center in the midst of any storm, and I could run to her for comfort. She made me feel complete and confident no matter how furious the tempest. She would often squeeze my hand and look me in the eye as if to say, "All will be well. Wait and see. I've got your back because you are mine."

Today without her on my side, I feel like an infantry battalion fighting in an open field without aerial cover, long-range artillery, or armored troops for combat support. I find myself vulnerable physically, emotionally, and spiritually because, in more ways than one, Mary gave me strength in all of these areas. She brought unique values into my life. I will forever be indebted to that jealously possessive and innocent high school girl who would not allow any other females to get too close to me. She did this simply by looking at them with eyes that spoke louder than words as if to say, "Keep off my possession. Wilfred is mine. Look elsewhere." Her rivals would become uncomfortable and leave us alone.

For forty years, from high school days, Mary worked persistently and patiently to bring order and to develop the best values in me, helping to reconcile the "all things are possible with the army" doctrine with the "we can do all things through Christ" creed. That is the Mary to whom I will always be indebted, the Mary who came into my life with a mission to bring about permanent change and harmony.

PART ONE

The First Five Years—
Courtship (1974-79)

CHAPTER 1

Meeting My High School Sweetheart

A DIVINE RELOCATION LEADS TO MY SOUL MATE

In May 1974 I reported to Nyandarua High School. I had just graduated from Narok Secondary School after taking my ordinary level exams (form four) and qualifying for entry into form five "A" levels. In those days, Kenya primarily used the British system of education with seven years of primary education followed by four years of secondary school and then two years of advanced level high school (A level or higher), similar to community college in the United States, Students could then enter the university for a degree course lasting a minimum of three years. The system was abbreviated as 7-4-2-3.

Nyandarua High school was a national mixed boarding school with a population of close to one thousand students, about 50–50 boys and girls. It also had a secondary section with forms one to four. Some forms had double or triple streams, but the higher section, forms five and six, had single streams. By the time I joined form five, Miss. Mary Mbuthuri was in her final year, form four. She had been at the school for most of her secondary education.

EVERYTHING ABOUT HER IS FABULOUSLY MYSTICAL

On the Sunday evening when I reported to school, clubs were meeting. As a born-again Christian, I wanted to know whether there was a Christian union. When I discovered that there was such a group, I went straight to the classroom where it was meeting. The chairman introduced me and two others new members to the brethren. We were given a chance to stand

3

and give our testimonies, but when my turn came, there was giggling, whispering, and excitement. This delighted many members, who took pride in their special guest. Members of other clubs had come that night for the first time out of fascination and curiosity. They wanted to see the cowboy/hippy dressed in a leather half coat over a long-sleeved shirt and bell-bottom pants, a three-inch-wide python-skin belt with an extra-large buckle mounted with two crossed pistols on the hips, and a pair of cowboy boots with wooden soles, wearing a watch on a two-inch-wide leather wristband and carrying a guitar in a special case—all custom-designed. It was not my intention to impress any one, I was just being myself and dressed in the same way I would often dress in my hometown Narok but things turned out different in Nyandarua environment.

After giving my testimony, I sang one of my favorite Christian songs, playing my guitar country style. It was like a storm hit the place with the ululation, wild clapping, and screams. But well into the meeting, something special caught my eye. The door slowly swung open, and like an angelic apparition, a cute young lady entered the meeting room. I could not keep my eyes off of the girl as she gingerly closed the door. *Lord Jesus!* I exclaimed inside, *what in the world am I looking at? This must be the most beautiful female I have seen anywhere. Certainly I have seen no one like her in my hometown, my home church, my former school, or the Christian youth camps I have frequented.*

Her face appeared to shine in the dimly lit room, and her beautiful, searching eyes sparkled like stars. Her pretty light skin could be seen on the small portions of her arms that weren't covered by the long-sleeved high-neck pullover she wore. She had short hair freshly curled for her sister's wedding, which she had attended that weekend, as I would learn later. She slowly tiptoed into the meeting as I watched in amazement, heading for a vacant bench in the aisle directly opposite from mine, and sat at the far end next to the wall, all the while careful not to disrupt the proceedings, create a fuss, or attract attention to herself. As she sat down, she pulled her dress in a womanly fashion to cover her beautiful legs below the knees. She followed intensely the events of the meeting but also kept scanning the room, noting the newcomers. She was a member and knew everybody else.

I kept looking in her direction, and I noticed that she was also looking in mine but with the corner of her eye as if she were spying on the uniquely dressed stranger across the aisle. She must have tried to figure him out, wondering, *Stranger, what's your name? And whence came you?* She had narrowly missed the initial self-introductions. She must have been asking herself what this hippy look-alike was doing at a Christian union meeting, a gathering of saints, not of hillbillies. *Judging by his attire, he surely can't belong here*, she must have thought. *Maybe he accidentally stumbled into this place, looking for the dancing club where he could play his guitar. He certainly does not look churchy like the rest of us here.* But she remained curious and may be concluded, *whatever the case may be, the young stranger is kind of cute, and I hope he can also sing some Christian music for heaven's sake.*

That stranger was Wilfred Nkoyo and the young beauty queen was none other than Miss. Mary Muthoni Mbuthuri, a recent Christian convert coveted by both Christian and non–Christian boys in Nyandarua and elsewhere where word of her conversion had spread. She sure was one of the most beautiful girls among the five hundred or so at the school. (Mary shared her thoughts about me from that night later during our courtship and even later in our married life this night would often become a subject of discussion between us.)

Before closing the meeting, the leader revisited the introductions, specifically recognizing the musical talent I had brought to the Christian union. "For those of you who just arrived," he said, "we have a new brother the Lord sent to our school just in time. He is a Maasai all the way from Narok." He took a long and discomfiting pause as latecomers started looking around, perhaps hoping to spot someone dressed in Shukas or Lesos, traditional Maasai wear consisting of two sheets made of cotton fabric, overlapped and crossed over the shoulders. They cover most of the upper body and no pants or under ware accompany the outfit. But the leader was facing in my direction, and my fancy dress betrayed me, making me the immediate suspect even though I was not dressed as expected.

"He loves the Lord with all his heart, and he is going to be a blessing to all of us," the leader continued. "He is also blessed with a talent in that he sings and plays a guitar, something we have always desired in our meetings." All this time, the beautiful angel listened intently and appeared composed. While others applauded loudly, she reacted with a gentle smile and with an air of dignity and as if she were asking, "How could that be?" Maybe she was wishing the stranger would open his mouth

5

and say something, whatever that might be. Unfortunately, by the time she arrived, I had already sung my best song and given my testimony, and because the meeting was almost over, there was no way I could have said anything more.

Inside of me, however, I felt a spark for that angelic girl. I thought I would not see her after the meeting since she had to rush to the girls' dormitory for the night, but I kept wishing I could do everything over again just for her. On our way out, several students crowded around me, wanting to shake hands, talk, and ask questions, but the reserved Mary was not the type to push through crowds for a moment of glory. Instead, she stood aloof with half a smile and her beautiful eyes trained on me while attentively listening to how I responded to the impromptu questions being fired at me from left and right. The questions covered everything, including my fancy shoes, my dress, my music, my conversion, and how I could claim to be a Maasai when I was not dressed like one. Mary was taking quiet notes in her mind, which she pondered during the night, as she told me later.

After the questions were exhausted, Mary shook my hand lightly, saying, "Good night, and God bless you, brother," in the most beautiful voice I had heard that evening. As I would eventually discover, Mary was the last to talk or to act in any situation, saying little and acting least. In the days and months that followed, many boys and girls, Christian and non-Christian, continued to show great curiosity and inquire about me. Mary had become a secret admirer who watched me from a safe distance, asking nothing but always giving me a beautiful, shy smile whenever our eyes would meet. The smile said, "I love you for me," speaking louder than any words could. In those days, there was a teaching among believers about calling things into existence and taking possession of them. It was based on Scripture, which tells of "the God who gives life to the dead and calls into being things that were not" (Romans 4:17 NIV).

Mary watched me from different angles (as she revealed years later)— from behind, from the sides, and at times from the window of her dormitory cubicle as I engaged boys and girls with the gospel along the pavements and the building corridors when they stopped me to discuss issues like dating between Christians. As time passed, Mary got a bit more comfortable with the "hippy guy," believing that he was a serious Christian man with a solid faith foundation and a mature understanding of Christians dating. That appraisal was based on the way I responded to this question and other doctrinal issues.

With every day that passed, Mary got a step closer, not realizing how proud and heroic that made me feel as this most coveted jewel appeared to be taking a keen interest on me. Other boys and girls were closely and enviously watching. But, unsure of who else had expressed interest in her and not wishing to create a commotion and confusion in the body of believers in a new environment, I tried to suppress and hide my daily increasing infatuation and fascination with the beauty queen. However, the more I tried to do this, the more she sought after me on the pretext of asking a question or two that she needed clarified. She would even send for me from the boy's dormitory or wherever I could be in the school compound, using a much junior Christian student called Paul who eventually became the most vital Runner-messenger between the two inseparable love-birds.

Over time, she disclosed to me the story of her last relationship, which dated back to her days before Christ, and how she ended it to give Christ first place in her life after she got born again. Apparently, her former boyfriend, the leader of the Christian union at the time, was a nominal Christian. He had graduated before I arrived. Mary was much younger and second year in secondary section of the school, nothing was serious or messy, especially with Mary. She told me the story after my clarification that Christians could date without falling into sin, she felt better about the issue. After that, she became one of many students who regularly consulted with me on areas of practical faith. In the end, Mary who had been drawn to me by her desire to know the truth became herself an expert on the issues thus teaming with me in responding to such needs. Things started developing fast and in line with God's plan for Mary and Wilfred.

CATCHING THE FISH WITH A GOLD COIN IN ITS BELLY

Through a faithful work of soul-winning at Nyandarua High School, God blessed me with a special catch, a fish with a golden coin in the belly.

That fish was none other than Miss. Mary Muthoni Mbuthuri, who would have a golden impact and sway on my life for four decades to come.

Mary was about to sit for her O levels, and having been an A student, she was sure of continuing in form five at any national school she desired. To no one's surprise, however, she chose to remain in the same school and to enroll in the same principle subjects as I had: mathematics, economics, geography, and general English paper. Her choice was a strategic move to create a way for us to regularly relate, and it worked as expected. We shared books and all our evening prep studies were held in the same room, my classroom. We shared a desk despite the fact that I was one class ahead of her. Only God knows how much time we spent reading and sharing notes compared with the time we spent gazing at and admiring each other.

During my two years at Nyandarua High School, we spent more than 80 percent of our free time around each other, either just two of us or in the company of other Christians or in the class studying side by side. A younger student named Paul as mentioned earlier, then in form one, was our mediator and runner-messenger. Mary would send him to look for me in the boys' dormitory or wherever I was on the vast campus to let me know that she was waiting for me in the matron's room or in a classroom, and I would rush there to be with her or else I would have to answer one commonly phrased question, "Where did you go?" This was always the hardest question for me to answer. I would try to say that I had been busy answering questions from my colleagues in the dormitory or getting cleaning done but the response was always the same: "But you are with those boys all the time day and night, yet my time with you is always limited to only a few day hours between breaks." But the truth was the exact opposite as stated above. Mary never had enough of me throughout her life and on the other hand I never had enough of Mary even now in her death. I always look forward to visit her grave, which I do regularly and I am glad I chose to affix my picture on the granite side by side with hers without apologies. Not that I worship Mary but I cannot remove the love seed she planted in me and neither can I think of anyone in this whole world who did so much, meant so much and still do than Mary even in her death. I struggle with the word death in describing Mary's status because she is still alive in my heart.

As our friendship grew, Mary no longer had time even for her classmate and best female friend, Martha. And whenever her father made one of his frequent visits to the school to see her and Mary was neither in class nor in her dormitory, would he inquire about "Wilfred, the young Maasai man from Narok." This was always the right move because Mary and I would then be found hanging out in the open football field sharing dreams or visiting with our Christian union sponsor at his house within the school compound having a Bible study fellowship or practicing singing together (see our pictures together in the picture section). Her father was always aware of this phenomenon and had no problem with it. He trusted, respected and loved Mary his daughter very much and had come to trust and respect me (Most of the pictures of us as students were taken outside this sponsor's house.)

Eventually we formed a duet, singing songs during Christian union meetings as I played my guitar. Mary was a wonderful soloist, a gift she developed in the Salvation Army church choir where she also learned to play the tambourine. We always looked forward to singing together. As she would confess years later after we got married, she always thought it a great privilege, honor and pride to sing with the stranger who had suddenly become a star and was so influential in the school, but then I would wonder whether she had any idea how proud I felt standing by her side or how much weight I attached to her being my fiancée, the girl so many boys in the school coveted and wished to win at any cost. Envy on me had spread across the Christian youth world of our time amongst those who knew of the beautiful Mbuthuri's conversion and now her new find. Some had it right that he was a modern fun loving Christian Brother from a dusty little town, Narok, in the middle of nowhere. Others had it all wrong that, this was a hippy crook with powers to play hypnotic mind-games and innocent Mary was just a victim caught up in the web. Yet God's favor required no effort on my part to hypnotize Mary or go about explaining all the mysteries about me. Things were falling into place according to His perfect plan. I could read envy on many faces, and I heard whispers whenever other students passed us on the sidewalks or while sitting in class at our regular "designated" study desk. This was a win-win situation, Mary won me and I won Mary. For Mary and me, the adoration lasted our whole lifetime together and those mysterious questions still linger in some minds to this day.

LEADERSHIP POSITIONS AS SCHOOL PREFECTS

Over the years that Mary was a student at Nyandarua, her no-nonsense leadership qualities had emerged, and so she was appointed one of the prefects in her dormitory. On the other hand, my influential status and leadership qualities had been quickly identified, and I was appointed a prefect in my dormitory soon after my arrival. Both of us now belonged to the Christian union and had become facilitators for the school administration as prefects (see our picture with other Christian leaders and prefects in the picture section). Prefect appointments came with privileges. All these involvements put together placed us in the limelight, especially in a mixed boarding school, which is like a large family. We became part of the spiritual and secular leadership.

MARY'S MOST JEALOUSLY GUARDED TREASURE

After these appointments, the time we spent together was never enough to satisfy our curiosity about each other. Whenever our break schedules coincided, we had to see each other even if we just shook hands and exchanged smiles for five minutes along the pavement it was still something to look forward to. It was an obsession. But a spark that started in me during the Christian union meeting when the angel tiptoed to a bench across the aisle from where I was sitting was about to burst into a flame that would remain burning for four decades. That happened in a room set aside as privileged space for prefects. It was a place for them to relax and do homework, to discuss issues of the day pertaining to prefect duties, or simply to hang out. Being prefects, we had access to the space at our convenience. It became our rendezvous point.

Otherwise, during regular evening prep times, Mary, who was in form four, would come to my class (form five) and sit next to me as if she needed help with homework but the truth was she just wanted to be next to the man she adore. She would walk majestically into the classroom straight to my desk at the back of the room, carrying her books and unconcerned about whoever was watching her. Out of amusement, my classmates, particularly boys, would turn their heads and follow her as she walked toward me and sat down next to me in a "reserved" seat. They would whisper but be sure that nobody heard what they said. They were also careful not to be too loud during preps otherwise they would end up with a write up from me or Mary for disturbing the peace because we were both prefects. Such a write up would result in a canning first thing the following morning or even suspension. Mr. Sam Kibe was a no nonsense principle of Nyandarua High in our days.

Mary would look at me with those large, innocent eyes, and careful not to disrupt other students in their study, she would smile passionately and whisper to me, "I've come." I would answer, "I'm here. I knew you were coming," and I would smile back. She would then open her textbook as if she were reading, but she was actually glancing at me with admiration every so often throughout the two-hour prep period. At the end of the period, when it was time to go to the dormitories, I would escort her as far as the no-trespass point for boys, and because we could not hug or kiss, we would shake hands. I made a habit of squeezing her hand just enough so she could scream a little for me but even then she would still not let me go easily. Finally, "Good night and God bless you" will be said over and over, in the end she would walk to her dormitory and from the upstairs window she would watch me walk all the way to the boys dormitory and she would be there to wave as I entered the dormitory. That was a daily ritual.

On a number of occasions, another girl, my classmate and secret admirer, referred to here only as Miss K, made an annoying habit of occupying the reserved seat at the designated desk. She did that often whenever we had a team assignment, using that as the excuse to sit next to me and to giggle the whole time. She always looked forward to such assignments, and she always chose to be on my team or pair with me no matter how hard I tried to avoid her, to avoid Mary's none verbal wrath. A cold war of some kind involving no smile and no curious gaze.

This was a source of great irritation to Mary. She would protest the following day or later that evening when we got together that I had allowed K to take her sacred spot. All this was done very politely, nothing loud or ugly which would be against her nature. She would always make a

11

statement and later in life I discovered this to be her way of making a protest statement, "I really think you like K a lot." I would explain that the problem had nothing to do with my liking for K but with a team assignment. However, no explanation would satisfy Mary. She would ask me why K was always my teammate and why the team didn't include other girls or was not entirely made up of boys. I would try to explain that K was responsible for picking her team and that apparently she always chose a team with me as a member. That was not satisfactory to Mary. And because Mary had to say good night to me daily, whenever K was sitting next to me, she would walk in a few minutes before the period was over, head straight for where we were sitting, and say in a clearly irate but peaceful voice, "I came to say good night." She would not greet or look at K, even after K converted; Mary saw that as a ploy to ingratiate herself with me and wouldn't recognize her as a sister in the Lord or welcome her in the fellowship of the brethren.

Eventually, Mary creatively devised a way to keep K off of the seat next to me. She would enter the classroom just before supper and place her books and her scarf on the seat. We would then go for supper, and as soon as the preps bell rang, Mary would head for the classroom and straight for the reserved seat and would sit down before I got there, preempting her rival. Even if we had a team project, she would sit next to me defiantly and get busy with her homework as the team discussed the work. And because Mary never talked to anyone else in the class besides me, no one would dare question her motive. In fact, everyone knew it. Besides, she was a prefect and had privileges to go to any class and do her preps and at the same time maintain order. My classmates would watch the love drama in silence, unwilling to make silly comments, to giggle, or to whistle because they feared Mary and respected both of us.

If for some reason I came in a few minutes late, Mary would ask me in a whisper, "Where did you go? I have been sitting here waiting for you all this time." I would apologize but she would not accept or reject my excuses. Not even the teaching staff or the principal dared comment on this mysterious bonding. This issue had come up in a school staff meeting at some point. The reason was because it was against the school's policy for this kind of intimacy but the agenda stalled as staff members after staff member wondered why Mary's father had not raised that concern and that whenever he visited he would be seen with both of us holding a lively conversation. The matter was shelved and never revisited. Instead, they all continued to watch the "inseparable couple" in wonderment.

In the end, the rendezvous point called the matron's room became a divine solution to the crowded classroom and Miss K's encroachment. It provided the privacy Mary and I needed to share our dreams. Unfortunately, it was available only over the weekends and parts of weekday evenings.

THE DIVINE RENDEZVOUS—THE MATRON'S ROOM, WHERE MARY SAID "YES"

The matron's room had become our best refuge despite occasional interruption by other prefects who came in and out, though that helped to keep our relationship open and healthy as a testimony to other students. Here we could talk to each other. One evening in this room, when it was just the two of us, I seized the opportunity. I will never forget this day for as long as I live, because with her *yes* Mary gave me a promise that would hold true for the next forty years. I asked, "Mary, would you consider giving your hand to me in marriage someday?" In keeping with her character, she calmly and firmly said, "Yes."

This word could have been engraved in stone. I would learn in later years that Mary's yes always meant yes and that her no always meant no. Mary wasn't easily swayed by contrary opinions or by events, and that is why her faith in Christ remained solid from the moment she said yes in 1973 to the day she went to meet Him in 2014. Mary might sometimes have appeared to change her position on an issue, but inside she remained unmoved. For example, after Mary became a born-again Christian in 1973, she made a major change in her life. She decided to end her relationship with a senior student, Mr. D, who had shown a lot of interest in her. A nominal Christian, he was chairman of the Christian union at Nyandarua High School. She told him that she had given her life to Jesus and could not continue their relationship.

After Mr. D graduated, he went to Switzerland to train in hotel management in the Kenyan tourism industry. When he returned in 1978, he came looking for Mary with many tears, hoping to persuade her to reconsider. However, perhaps unknown to him, Mary was already committed to an intense relationship with me. He appealed to Mary's older sister to intervene because she was aware of their past relationship and was hosting Mary in her family apartment in Madaraka Estates in Nairobi at the time. Hoping she could help, the sister said he could come to her home at a time when Mary would be returning from work, but the moment Mary arrived to find Mr. D sitting on a sofa, she made an about turn and left the apartment, according to what Mary told me.

Mr. D was disappointed but never gave up on this irresistibly beautiful young woman, especially now she was a working girl and looking elegant. He came from a wealthy and influential family and now had a management position in the hotel industry. Mr. D thought he could use that in his favor. He gathered the courage to visit Mary's parents in their rural home, hoping to woo them with a serious dowry offer, but Mary left home that day, unwilling to consent to the deal. She wouldn't participate regardless of who supported the plan, and the project collapsed.

These dramatic events took place while I was in Pakistan on military training in 1978. Nothing could change Mary's no to yes. Material considerations or status could never influence her decision. Mary had given her heart, 100% to me, and even if all she had was photographs of me, and the promises I made to her in 1974 during our high school days, she was determined to wait for me, convinced that I was God's choice for her and that I was a believer of like faith. She had come to love me with all her mind, soul, and spirit. Though some members of her family viewed Mary's choice as immature and lacking wisdom, her faith in me and willingness to wait only increased. She proved them all wrong because she was a prayerful woman who never doubted God's will and purpose for her. During our early years of courtship, Mary often told me that her greatest dream was that she would marry someone who would serve alongside her as a minister of the gospel. According to Mary, that man was Wilfred and not Mr. D despite his wealth and family status. That was Mary's hallmark: faithfulness to a commitment.

Mary was a person of few words, but they were always well thought out. She also strived to avoid contradicting herself by saying one thing one day and another the next. And Mary was a woman of her word. When she promised to marry me, all these virtues came into play. Times changed, and her lover was off in another country; she was pressured by relatives to reconsider Mr. D, but Mary's position remained constant against all other variables. Her yes remained in force until she said "I do" on October 13, 1979, in the presence of an overflow crowd at the Pentecostal Assemblies of God church in the dusty little town Narok but in the most colorful military wedding yet, to this day. She married me and remained faithful to the day she looked at me for the last time. After I had finished massaging her back and neck, she thanked me as always and said her last "good-night and God bless you my beloved" on June 4, 2014, at around 1:30 a.m.

MARY'S LOVE TOTALLY IMMERSED IN ONE MAN FOR FORTY YEARS

Throughout our high school days, during Mary's years of work in Nairobi before we got married, and during our thirty-five years of marriage, there was never a day when I felt threatened by a competitor. That was true when I was in the country with her or outside the country and when she was in America alone (at 28) with our children or on her own (at 36). Mary was always a one-boy girl as a single and after marriage, a one-man married woman, content and totally committed physically, emotionally, and spiritually to me. She was consumed on daily basis by love for me. This love needed no words because it was evident in all her actions whether in my presence or my absence. She proudly and jealously guarded her status as my woman "Mrs. Nkoyo", treasuring it to her last breath. In return, I made Mary my everything besides God and she knew that.

All this became clear during her last week of life in the intensive care unit at Baylor Medical Center in Irving, Texas. During that short time, seven days, whenever she could not verbalize her adoration, anytime I entered her room, Mary's blood pressure and heart rate would normalize, and her face would glow with life, joy, and hope. A smile would come to her lips, and her eyes would sparkle, overflowing with love and admiration for me. These mysterious events took place to the consternation of nurses and doctors, her sister Elizabeth, and our daughter Caroline. Mary would turn her head in the direction of my voice and gaze at me as I approached her bed. When I would tease her by saying I had come to take her home, she would attempt to sit up and stretch her arms toward me, just like a baby responding to a parent, as if saying, "Here I am, my love. I am ready to go with you wherever you want to take me." These were emotional and very intense moments.

Over the years, Mary's love was always evident in her beautiful, penetrating eyes, which kept a constant watch on me, especially when circumstances separated us. Her eyes always spoke to me more clearly than any words could concerning the way she felt about situations and issues. She reminded me of my late mother. When I was a little boy, my mother loved me with a passion. She would take me with her everywhere she went and remotely controlled my behavior solely through eye contact. She did not even need to be with me. I thought that she was omnipresent and was watching me. I loved her very much and feared to do wrong because she would never spare me.

Mary's eyes had a different appeal. They said, "I love you and only you. I have never loved or desired another besides you. As I have remained faithful to you, remain faithful to me." With this haunting message, if I was near another woman, something would tell me, "Look away," and I would do so immediately. If I was about to say something intended to arouse a lady's affection, something would say, "Reserve that for Mary because Mary would not say that to any man but you." Whether Mary was healthy and attractive or she was down and out with depression and emotionally unresponsive, these words held true. For the forty years we spent together, we left no space for anyone but each other.

This obsession had its roots in high school. Mary loved and trusted me, and in return I loved and trusted her. We were consumed with one another. We tended to think the same way and often anticipated what the other was about to say. Mary would express an opinion and ask, "What do you think?" I would simply concur. Our relationship had taken a brother-sister character. Her relatives were not in-laws to me, and neither were my relatives her in-laws. My brothers were her brothers, my sisters her sisters, my parents her parents, and vice versa. This oneness became a hallmark of our marriage.

INTRODUCING MARY TO MY PEOPLE

Soon after Mary said she would marry me, we decided to reveal our relationship to our parents and relatives, my pastor, and Christian friends outside the school. We planned to go on a mission to the Maasai land, my home district, over the school Christmas break of 1974. During that time I would introduce my girlfriend to all my relatives, my Christian friends, and my home church. The outreach mission, sponsored by the Full Gospel Churches of Kenya, covered many urban and trading centers. The climax of the mission was in my hometown, Narok. I was the chief speaker at a massive crusade in the marketplace. Mary led the prayer of repentance and prayed for new converts and the sick.

In that simple setting, God did mighty things. A boy, fourteen years old crippled with polio from childhood suddenly started walking without aid of his crutches. Many of the sick started giving testimonies of healing. Before long, there was a commotion as people surged toward the little makeshift platform, asking to receive Christ as their savior. My father, a stubborn critic of Christianity and a doubting Thomas on whether I would remain a Christian, gave his life to Christ with many tears as he witnessed the crippled boy, whom he knew, throw away his crutches and for the first time walk unsupported. My sister and my uncles also got converted, and my mother soon followed.

The events of December 1974 became a reference point for many years thereafter. That three-day hometown crusade confirmed the call that God had placed on our lives as a couple.

After that crusade, I did not need to introduce my girlfriend. Our friends and relatives were already convinced that God had a great plan for us as a couple. The results of this first outreach helped define everything that followed in our lives until the last day of our forty years of love and friendship. We discovered how well we complemented each other in our spiritual gifts. I could preach a powerful faith- building message, Mary would follow with a potent prayer, and great things would happen due to our agreement. We also sang together and stirred many through our music. Henceforth, most of our friends, especially the elderly folks, started referring to Mary as "Mary wa Nkoyo" meaning, Mary of Nkoyo.

Initially outwardly we shied off from the title but eventually became proud and accustomed to it. This was especially true for Mary, as she would tell me years after we were married. We could hear the title murmured among older folk whenever we visited home churches, way before we were engaged. Our situation was uncommon in those days because church elders taught that unmarried people could not date since they would easily fall into sexual temptations. The Full Gospel Churches in particular held to this teaching and vigorously enforced to the point of expelling youth who showed dating tendencies. But our relationship had set a revolution in motion in this respect, a similar phenomenon that followed in Nyandarua High school after the dilemma that faced the authorities as the staff tried to deliberate on the issue of our relationship but instead ended up relaxing a rule that for years was often enforced through corporal punishment or suspension from school. Now in the Christian community to which we belonged, we were viewed as a model and occasionally invited to minister as a dating couple. I will discuss in more detail the bonds between Mary and my immediate family, especially my mother, who passed on to glory in Mary's loving arms. The acceptance of Mary by my family and my church gave a major boost to our relationship for the rest of our life together. Mary won acceptance by my people from the first day they met her, she became one of their own, thus making me a debtor to them as if owing her to them. Any time I met them while alone, they wanted to know of Mary's welfare and even as I cared for Mary during her struggles with health issues, they always wanted to be in the know about her progress because she had become essentially part of them. In a huge way, that sense of indebtedness translated to purpose that drove our marriage for decades.

MARY BRINGS ME TO KNOW HER RELATIVES

Back in Nyandarua high school days. In January 1975, we started outreach missions to the outlying areas from our school, but even as part of a school team, Mary and I always paired together going from house to house witnessing. Our friendship continued to grow as our joint ministry strengthened. During April school break that year, Mary took me to her home where she let me blend in with her family. Her older brother Peter, who had loved music from his days in the Salvation Army church that the family attended, would play his guitar. He was a professional musician. We became instant friends, and forty years later that relationship remains rock solid. We would play guitars together and sing with Mary on the tambourine.

Mary's parents were equally receptive of me. Over the years, they had become used to receiving friends of their sons and daughters in their home, since their ministry involvement kept streams of outsiders visiting with some staying on. They had an open-door policy. Their children were free to associate with anybody without suspicion or questions by their parents. I found this encouraging. In time, I became a frequent and special guest at Mary's home. Her mother would fondly introduce me to other visitors as one of her sons. I became an adopted member of the family, Mary's other brother. I grew to love the Mbuthuris and would visit them during school breaks. Mary's home in Chokereria near Gilgil was closer to our school than my hometown Narok was and became my first stop on the way there.

Once with Mary's family, I was home and secure and never wanted to leave. She was beautiful and loving, and we were obsessed with each. She would treat me like her own brothers, her parents were trusting, and Peter had become like a blood brother to me. Their home became my second home. I was like a twin brother to Mary. We were the same size and height, and even though her skin was much lighter, wherever we went in the mission field, strangers thought we were blood relatives, especially because of the way we treated one another. We would walk in neighboring villages, sharing our dreams of what we wanted to become someday.

All these dreams came to pass before Mary left for glory. I have written this book as a way of counting our blessings and telling the world what Mary contributed toward their fulfillment. I am indebted to her and to her people, who unselfishly let her become part of me, making me complete. She transformed my entire being. Besides God, my maker, I owe to Mary everything I ever accomplished and became in life from the day she said yes in high school. Her virtues enhanced mine.

BEGINNING AN ARMY CAREER

In the coming pages I will highlight my military career of twelve years, its merits and demerits, and how it impacted my marriage. Fellow officers and other army colleagues were instrumental in our wedding, and I am forever indebted to them for the role they played. I owe my spouse to them considering that the groom party, led by my best man and in full military ceremonial uniform complete with ceremonial swords, traveled for miles to be there for us at our wedding. An advance preparation party made up of men from my immediate squadron (part of the 66 Artillery Regiment) had moved to our wedding venue three days in advance. My army career led me to discover a new loving family, one that cared for me and about me, and when Mary came into my life, she became part of that family. I always owed her to my army family, and that realization continually inspired purpose in our marriage even long after I voluntarily retired.

PART TWO

From "I Do" to the First Storm Front (1979–92)

CHAPTER 2

Building a Career and a Family

LOVE TILL DEATH DO PART

While I served in the Kenyan army artillery, based in Gilgil, and Mary worked for an insurance company in Nairobi, our friendship continued to grow strong and become more focused. In October 1979, when I was a substantive lieutenant, Mary and I tied the knot in a wonderful military wedding conducted in my rural home church by the Rev. Joseck Omogotu. This pastor had led me to Christ in Narok nine years earlier. Our wedding was the first military wedding and the largest that the people of Narok had witnessed. These same people had seen the first sizable miracle crusade ever conducted in Narok, which Mary and I had led five years earlier as young adults in high school.

At last the angelic girl whom I had seen almost six years earlier in a dimly lit meeting room in high school was mine to have and to hold. The date was October 13, 1979, an odd one for superstitious folks, but to those of the household of faith, this was the day He had ordained for us five years earlier when Mary said, "Yes, I will," in response to my question whether she would considering marrying me someday. She had spoken in the future tense in the matron's room in 1974, but this day she would speak in the present tense as she said, "Yes, I do."

Those words gave birth to a covenant between Mary and me, signed in the presence of hundreds of witnesses. We were to detach ourselves from the most important entities in our lives, our parents, and become fused permanently to each other. Scripture says, "Therefore shall a man leave his father and his mother, and shall cleave unto his wife: and they shall be one flesh" (Genesis 2:24 KJV). Though the verse points to only one actor, man, the action applies to both man and woman, and actually, the woman's move is more dramatic and public.

Mary's father walked her down the aisle and handed her to me. Mary made a greater sacrifice than I did because on top of leaving her mother and father, she dropped the name of the person who bore her and raised her in favor of mine, ceasing to be Miss Mary Muthoni Mbuthuri and becoming Mrs. Mary Muthoni Nkoyo. In essence she lost her lifelong identity and assumed mine. Her father, my best friend, walked her down the aisle, guiding her with his hand to her future. His hand and lips were trembling, a natural reaction for a loving parent parting with his daughter. He placed Mary's beautiful hand gently in mine without a word, but his body language clearly said to me, "I hand to you my most treasured jewel, my baby girl, beautiful and without a physical or emotional scar. I have nurtured her to the best of my ability, and it behooves you to keep things the same or better."

This event took place in the presence of hundreds of people from different parts of the country, Christians and non-Christians, who watched every step as father and daughter walked slowly down the aisle. This momentous occasion laid a great sense of responsibility upon my heart and created a strong feeling of indebtedness in me. A voice seemed to say, "You owe this girl to her loving father, who brought her into existence inside her mother's womb and who nurtured her from a baby into this beautiful girl who has attracted you and loved you adoringly. No trust could equal this that a man should turn over his life's greatest treasure to a stranger like you. You are a debtor to him henceforth in the way you treat her as long as she lives with you."

I relived that moment again and again, especially when Mary was at the lowest point in her struggle with depression, completely detached emotionally. And from that voice I would get the inspiration to fight the good fight for Mary, doing so with her father's interests in mind, certain that he would never have given up on her or spared anything, including his own life, for his daughter. At that instant, Mary would take the form of a baby girl with me as her daddy. It was now my turn to rise to the occasion to care for "my most treasured jewel." I would feel a strong urge to do my utmost best in honor of the man who by faith entrusted his daughter to me and to whom I was forever indebted. That sense of indebtedness strengthened the purpose of my marriage and my commitment to Mary for all the years we were together.

The phrase "becoming one flesh" in Genesis suggests a type of fusion, defined in the online Merriam-Webster dictionary as "a distinct entity formed by the combining of two or more different things" (http://www. merriam-webster.com/thesaurus/fusion). Our covenant implied that we had committed to becoming one distinct entity, the product of a chemical combination of two separate entities, Wilfred Nkoyo and Mary Mbuthuri, and that only death could unwrap this mix. We willingly entered into that covenant, vowing to stick together, to sink or float together in sickness or in health, in poverty or in plenty, until death did us part. But even death has been thus far unable to take away the love seed Mary planted in me because while Mary has passed according to many, she is still alive in my heart.

We did this in the presence of hundreds of people. Surely, few if any covenants between two souls involve so many witnesses. I vowed to love and to cherish Mary in health or in sickness until she or I died. She did the same. On that day at that little church in my hometown, hundreds of friends from all walks of life and from both of our families converged. They all came to witness the beginning of a journey that day by day, mountain by mountain, and valley by valley would help build a solid family, a successful career, and a ministry within a marriage between one man and one woman guided by a purpose anchored in a sense of indebtedness to all those witnesses. We remained faithful to each other and to our witnesses until death did us part. We owed it to them. With God's help and their prayers, we delivered.

CHAPTER 3

My Military Career Offers Mary a Gospel Mission Field

Our military wedding in Narok initiated Mary into a new family to which she completely adapted, spirit, soul, and mind. And while military life can be stressful to marriages and families, Mary saw an opportunity to reach out in this wide and ready mission field. While I was rising in my career as a military officer, my wife found her calling, reaching families left behind in the barracks by husbands on deployment and bringing the comforting message of the gospel.

Military families are stressed to the maximum limit due to the demands of the service on soldiers and officers. The frequent cross postings, overseas deployments, and other field operational duties that take men and women away for prolonged periods place intense strain on their spouses and even lead to the breakup of marriages. The demands of military service often compete with a marriage commitment, and for the most part, the former wins, often in more ways than one: cases of infidelity, drug abuse, alcoholism, suicide, and depression abound amongst military families. Children rebel when one of the parental figures becomes a prolonged absentee, adding to stress in a marriage. All these more often than not lead to separation or divorce. The impact on the family may be direct or indirect, but service personnel have little say concerning transfers or field deployment.

Over the years that I served, I saw the careers of good friends and of my own soldiers get in the way of their marriages and families. Having held direct command of service personnel or been responsible for administration, I can say that all the issues in soldiers' lives, outside of the operational ones, were directly or indirectly related to their immediate or extended families.

They involved what we called a soldier's welfare. And in the end, every operational issue was directly or indirectly affected by a soldier's welfare. Soldiers and officers either lost their families, or their spouses led secret adulterous lives or became depressed and turned to alcohol and drugs due to frustrations. I knew of children of soldiers who ended up in trouble with the law as a result of their fathers' prolonged absences. The shocking dark sides of supposedly most successful military careers became public through family members who could no longer live in hiding. These tragic tales came as a surprise to admirers of highly decorated service personnel who led double lives causing deep and permanent wounds to their spouses

OUR LIFE MORE STABLE THAN MANY OTHERS

I was blessed during my twelve-year military career. I spent short periods away from my family while on training or while training others in field operations, but a great percentage of my service life was spent close to my family at the home base assigned to staff duties. Even though one of our two children was born while I was away on a military exercise, God was good to us and our children grew up with me around. I was rarely posted out of my unit. The few times I relocated, I did so with my family and was able to find housing for married officers before moving to my new post. For example, when I was posted to a Nairobi-based Air Cavalry battalion in 1980, I moved from a mansion in Gilgil, where I served with an Artillery brigade, to a mansion in the Langata barracks, where my family lived from 1980 to 1982.

The greatest move that I made in my career as a married officer came at the end of 1982 when I was appointed the assistant military attaché to the United States and sent to Washington, D.C., more than ten thousand miles from Kenya. The best part was that I moved with my family. Caroline and Armstrong were only two years and two months, respectively. The fact that we always lived together as a family helped us adjust smoothly to new environments. In the United States, we were able to create our own small world thousands of miles away from our cultural comfort zone. We remained in America until 1984, and when we returned, we found another mansion in Gilgil barracks readily.

When I retired in 1988, my family made a smooth transition to civilian life because we had become accustomed to living together without much separation and disruption while in the service. God was gracious, allowing us to develop a strong relationship as a couple while bonding with our children over those years in the military. There was a divine purpose in the stability we enjoyed and in the rare opportunity Mary had to develop a ministry among spiritually needy military families. That stability while in active service became very beneficial to us as a couple after retirement giving us a smooth resettlement and reentry into a civilian life, it felt very much like a continuation.

OUR MINISTRY IN THE ARMED FORCES

The organizational structure and operational doctrine of the Kenyan armed forces are patterned after the British system. Through the chaplaincy branch, an integral part of Kenya armed forces, officers, servicemen, and their families come together to worship and to express their faith freely. Two main Christian denominations, Roman Catholicism and Protestantism, are officially represented, with churches in almost every barrack manned by Catholic and Protestant chaplains. The Islamic faith is also represented, with mosques manned by Maalims. The padres, priests, and Maalims are commissioned officers under special services and are paid by the government, which also pays for the construction and operational costs of places of worship.

The Military Christian Fellowship of Kenya (MCFK), an independent fraternity fully endorsed by the armed forces, operates in cooperation with the chaplaincy. The MCFK is an affiliate of the International Military Christian Fellowship with chapters wherever freedom of religion in the armed forces is enshrined in law. The organization is mainly administered by retired Christian armed forces personnel. Officers in active service also participate as officials. The latter conduct the activities of the MCFK, such as Bible studies, in the barracks.

The chaplaincy and the MCFK became special to me and my wife. We actively participated in both; I was an active uniformed official of the MCFK, and as a couple we supported the work of the chaplain in every barrack where we lived. I had joined the armed forces as a committed Christian, and these two organizations gave me a sense of purpose, belonging, and spiritual nurturing, all which I greatly needed. When I married Mary in 1979, she found a rich mission field, and through the chaplain, she started women's fellowships, reaching many officers' and soldier's wives. My wife and I also travelled overseas, representing the MCFK in 1987, a tour sponsored by the American Military Christian Fellowship (AMCF).

I had other rare opportunities during my Christian life in the military. As a member of the MCFK, I held Bible study sessions with officers and servicemen in tents in the field and in our home in the barracks. We did this weekly. Many gave their lives to Christ through such moments. For Mary, armed forces life was a time of spiritual enrichment and growth as we shared our faith in a unique setting or a mission field.

This experience created a long-lasting bond between my family and service personnel and their families. In 1990, two years after my retirement from the service, when we held a huge three-day open-air crusade in Gilgil, where I was based for eight out of my twelve years, almost half of the crowd was made up of my former soldiers and their families. They had seen our names on the posters circulated in the town, and they came out in big numbers. As we made altar calls, soldiers would surge to the platform in scores, wailing and calling out my name, it was a very humbling experience. Seeing the faces of many servicemen who served under my command received Christ in those three days, especially as they witnessed the miracles God was performing. The most dramatic involved a woman who arrived on crutches and started walking lifting them up high above her head after a prayer of faith. She had been a victim of a multiple car accident that left her legs crippled. She could not walk without her crutches and help from friend that brought her to the crusade ground (see pictures of this eventful crusade in the picture section)

Mary shined as a minister of the gospel and represented the best model of a Christian officer's wife and mother among many others. In 1986, our daughter Caroline at the age of six was chosen to present a bouquet of flowers to HE the President Daniel Arap Moi, the commander in chief of the armed forces, during an international conference organized by the AMCFK in Nairobi. Accompanying our daughter on this memorable occasion, Mary shook hands with the president, as did I as one of the organizers. In a way, this was a recognition of our ministry among uniformed personnel. In a dramatic follow-up to that successful event, the AMCF (USA), which co-sponsored the Nairobi conference, sponsored Mary and me on a one-month tour of the United States in June 1987. We visited several chapters of the AMCF, and all our expenses were covered (see pictures of the conference activities in the picture section)

The military service created unique opportunities for us to grow spiritually, to serve the spiritual needs of servicemen and officers, and as a result to enhance the purpose of our union as a married couple.

RETIREMENT FROM MILITARY SERVICE; MARY'S CAUTIOUS COUNSEL

By nature, Mary was a deep well of wisdom. She had also sharp intuition and a quick analytical mind and could see the fault lines in presentations and would advise that we move with caution on certain commitments. She would spot details deliberately left out of an offer and reveal them to me later, saying, "That person told us only what he wanted us to hear and not what we needed to know." Her counsel on such matters was dependable and weighed heavily in many decisions I made. This did not come easily for me, but after several failures resulting from decisions I made against her counsel, I learned the hard way never to ignore her advice. With time I would solicit her opinion before making major decisions.

Mary was fully aware of how much her counsel influenced my choices. However, she never tried to use her intuitive advantage to manipulate me or take that dependence as a sign of weakness in the man of the house. She didn't want the glory or to be in the limelight as the family spokesperson unless I let her. Instead she chose to remain in the background and respectfully in our privacy cautioning me against taking an offer or committing myself. We would step aside from where she would give me her honest opinion in a complimentary way, leaving me to consider all the options based on alternative views. She was that sharp but in the end, Mary would let me make the final decision. When we succeeded in a venture based on her advice, she never beat her chest but graciously wanted us to share in the glory.

Mary had humility and patience, accommodating my daring nature in risky ventures. When I stubbornly insisted on a plan of action (as I often did), she would do everything she could to help, to the extent of financing projects whose outcome she doubted. If I failed, she would lift me up, dust me off, and console me, saying, "I came on board so I could be with you at this moment. I expressed my doubts to you from the beginning because I sensed in my spirit that even though the plan was sound, the timing was not right. However, my love, we must move on and wait for the timing of God. We might have rushed ahead of Him. Remember that your last great victory came because you patiently waited."

God had favored me with a loving spouse who affirmed me even when I had fallen flat on the ground and who was gracious enough to reach out and lift me up and to restore my fractured wings so I could again fly like an eagle. Mary's commitment moved her to say, "Although I cannot stop you from embarking on this doubtful venture, I will follow you so when you need me I will be by your side. I will never let you walk alone even if I have to follow blindly." That passionate love covered my faults and healed my wounded pride whenever I crash-landed in my wild pursuit of excellence. This was Mary's attitude, never condemning, never shaming or "I told you" remarks. Her positive attitude and sensitivity to my manhood reinforced the purpose that drove our marriage. I owe everything I am and accomplished in life to Mary's counsel, affirmations and prayers which always bridged the gaps left in my many plans of action over the years in our married life

This blind trust and commitment would face a maximum test when one day early in 1988 I came home from the office and told Mary that I had decided to take early retirement from the army. This was a risk way beyond her wildest dreams. My decision came at a prime age of thirty four and stage of my career at the rank of a major when Mary saw only smooth sailing ahead, especially for her ministry interests in the military mission field. But as far as I was concerned, the time had come to leave and to start afresh after twelve years. I had a strong witness in my spirit that our family should get ready for the next mountain in our life and that we needed to prepare for it under a different environment from the military one. I had been promoted to the rank of a major, a springboard to unlimited opportunities in the army. My career had brought me great advantages, I was uniquely favored in every turn and stage, right from my days in college as a junior officer cadet. I still remember how I was chosen as one of the three best cadets after our basic training, to proceed to the Royal Military Academy in Sand Hurst, England where we were supposed to proceed with our advance military officer's training but just before I could start preparing to leave the country, another yet more coveted opportunity came up and I was again selected with two other cadets to meet and receive special Awards from the Head of State during our commissioning parade. Innumerable unique favors came my way in the course of my life of military service, pointing to what perhaps future may have held for me. As a captain in the army, soon after the attempted military coup led by Kenya air force, having just graduated from the School of aviation as an Air traffic Controller, I was given the appointment to take over from the disbanded Air force, a post as in-charge of Kenya Airspace security operating from Jomo Kenyatta International Airport Nairobi but that appointment was superseded by the next appointment that landed on my desk a few days later as Assistant Military Attaché based in Washington DC (read about that in coming pages). But, in spite of all these favors, certain things within the system were becoming moral hindrances to me even as I rose in ranks and responsibility and I was not ready to compromise.

I had just daringly redressed or complained about my brigade commander to the army commander on one such matter. I wanted to be reassigned to another brigade, but the results fell short of my expectations. I resolved to resign even though without a solid plan for my next move. I drafted my resignation letter and shared the matter with Mary my confidant and counsel. Fully aware of my boldness, she was afraid I was going to submit the letter soon after I shared the plan with her. She asked if she could pray over the matter for a few months and let God speak to her on this weighty matter. I let her take her time. But a day after I returned from a month's assignment at an artillery school located in a remote district where I was training noncommissioned officers, Mary broke the surprising news to me in her hallmark style. She said, "My beloved, I have been fasting and praying about your resignation plan, and I am at peace with it. I have witnessed in my spirit that truly this is our time to move on to our next appointment and destiny." I may never know fully how that one month separation contributed to Mary conviction, but certainly it did and I wasted no time to act.

I asked her to accompany me in delivering the application to the army commander at the army headquarters in Nairobi because I knew he would not consider my application or let me go home without her consent. She was agreeable and we both left Gilgil to deliver the application. Mary did not have to appear before him, but when he inquired about her and the family, I assured him that she was in our car waiting outside in case he wanted her opinion on the matter but reluctantly, he let me go saying to me in a fatherly way that the door would remain open for me if my plans did not work. I saluted him and left.

My decision had an enormous impact on our family, coming at a huge price and demanding sacrifice. It called for supernatural courage on my part and required Mary to hear from God. I was ending a twelve-year military career at the prime age of thirty-four. Mary was thirty-two, a homemaker with two young children (Caroline, eight, and Armstrong, six). Though I had no clear plan and my decision carried huge unknown implications, I had a deeply rooted conviction to follow my conscience and to let God provide along the path. He proved faithful from the beginning 1988 to this moment as I write. A few highlight have been shared in the following chapters.

In retrospect, that risky plunge into the unknown was the only option that would have allowed us to follow God's larger plan for us. We needed freedom to choose a country where we could do more ministry, but the path to that freedom was getting narrower with my rise in the military ranks. I did not know all the details of the plan, but involving Mary was extremely important because I knew she would pray and get a clearer confirmation, which she did. Her willingness to plunge with me hand in hand into a precarious future became the ultimate test of Mary's faith in God and trust in me as her husband. She remained steadfast despite my stubborn character, which in the past had gotten the best of me. God gave me Mary to balance this part of myself.

In August 1988 my application was finally granted, and we left the military barracks soon after that for Limuru in the Kiambu district where within a year we opened a cafeteria we called the Heritage Inn. This became the base for our outside catering business. We mainly delivered hot lunches to the surrounding schools to kids whose parents had to pre-pay for the service at the cafeteria. By late 1989, we had become a household name among hundreds of families that wanted hot lunches for their schoolchildren in Limuru and the outlying areas. We also catered major functions such as weddings, graduations, and political dinners.

Limuru was a new town to our family. I hailed from Narok and Mary from Gilgil, but this was the place God had planned that we would start a new life. He would give us favor and acceptance. We prospered and rented a huge mansion on a tea plantation. The property was meant for a plantation manager. We made it the headquarters for our evangelistic ministry, Christian Heritage Ministries International Inc. From here, we were free to go out and do evangelistic crusades around the country (see pictures of the mansion and the origins of tent ministry in the picture section)

But God's ultimate plan was yet to be revealed. He wanted to move our family from Kenya entirely and bring us to a new inheritance as citizens of the United States, according to His word spoken to us in Limuru in 1989 (Deuteronomy 6:10–11). This would never have happened had I continued to rise in the army ranks and to prosper in any other business ventures in Kenya. Even in Limuru, where we were deeply entrenched in a successful catering business, God had to pluck us out violently but unscathed in 1990. This was a dramatic and traumatic experience but a miraculous one, which you will read about later in this book. Finally, at the end of our wilderness wanderings and according to His ultimate plan, we landed in the United States of America on August 14, 1992, exactly four years after I exited the army. In a purpose-driven marriage, agreement became our source of courage in making successful decisions even when the path was foggy and our destiny uncertain, God honored courage, boldness and agreement. Where there is agreement there is power.

CHAPTER 4

Mary's Prayers shielded me from a Certain Death Trap (1982-84)

Mary was an independent and reliable intellectual and a spiritual powerhouse. From the day we got married, my love for her and my confidence in her wisdom and judgment continued to grow. With time, I became convinced that Mary could be entrusted to make all decisions pertaining to our family welfare and could give me the best counsel in moments of crises, enabling me to reach sound decisions. She was always current, articulate, and detailed on every issue in our lives. She always remained focused and unperturbed by disruptions when working on a solution to any issue be it economic, social, or spiritual.

Mary did not have to write things down. She had a sharp memory and could recall in great detail all past significant events, where they took place, and any special circumstance at the time. She would then draw lessons from those experiences and apply them to the immediate challenge. Mary would thoroughly test the validity of her views in her mind before she spoke. She often kept me in suspense, unsure where she stood on issues that I thought required a quick response. She never had answers at her fingertips. Mary pondered her responses in her heart and refined them in her mind before verbalizing them.

This phenomenon was amplified many times over during her down times with depression. She would be withdrawn and uncommunicative for many months, yet I was always aware of how active her heart and mind were every waking moment. She kept detailed records on our family friends and made it a point to touch base with them and get regular updates and because of that, we were able to maintained contact with most of our acquaintances going back to the early years of our courtship. To

Mary, friends were treasures for keeps. They were a major part of her life, and she always took interest in what happened to them. She would often call them for words of comfort, and whenever she needed help in prayer support, they were trusted allies.

All these virtues converged when Mary was subjected to a maximum test, left all alone in Washington, D.C., unable at first to find out why her husband had suddenly been recalled from his post in the United States and was more than ten thousand miles away in Nairobi, Kenya.

It all started on Monday morning, May 7, 1984, when I was suddenly recalled from my Foreign Service post in Washington as an assistant defence attaché. Mary was left behind with two little children and the responsibility to pack all of our belongings and follow me to Kenya because I would not be returning to the United States. I left Washington in a matter of hours that evening after calling Mary around ten o'clock that morning from my office to inform her of my imminent departure.

Mary would show her reliability, wisdom, and moral courage in making tough decisions in a hostile environment created by the male chauvinists behind my sudden recall based on charges of treason that they fabricated against me, hoping to end my career and to destroy me. They were naïve about who Mary was and about how she would respond when push came to shove. To them she was just a timid little African village woman, the kind they pushed around in their towns or offices, using their positions. Little did they know that Mary was independent and intellectually sharp and a spiritual powerhouse and that nobody was going to mess with her, her family, or her family belongings.

Mary's heroic face-off with Lieutenant Colonel W, defence attaché in Washington, and Mr. G., Kenya's acting ambassador in Washington, must have lingered vividly in their minds for some time after she finally boarded a flight with her children in tow and with keys to a shipping container and all the documents pertaining to her family belongings (both in America and in West Germany) in her pockets. She left the United States on the day and time of her choice and on her terms.

In retrospect, I thank God that He chose Mary and not me, to show His might in this confrontation. I have chosen this story out of many because of its magnitude and to illustrate the truth of God's Word that whatever the Enemy may mean for evil, He will turn it for our good.

Scripture says, "And we know that all things work together for good to them that love God, to them who are the called according to his purpose" (Romans 8:28 KJV).

GOD'S FAVOR DEFIES YEARS OF HUMAN LABOR

My first visit to the United States came during my tour as the assistant military attaché at the Kenyan Embassy in Washington. I was a twenty-eight-year-old army captain. I had just finished training as an air traffic controller and hoped to serve overseeing Kenya's airspace security from the airspace radar room based at Jomo Kenyatta International Airport in Nairobi. Within a matter of days, I had been offered two appointments by the Kenyan Department of Defence (DOD), and I opted for the more coveted and privilege-loaded one, a diplomatic post at the Kenyan embassy in Washington. I was to be accompanied by my Mary (twenty-six), Caroline (two), Armstrong (only two-and-a-half months old), and a nanny, who would help care for our little children.

The DOD fast-tracked documentation because of the short notice we were given to prepare to relocate. The appointment was to last for at least two years and could be extended for another two. My job was administration of the military section at the embassy, mainly dealing with hundreds of military students training across the United States and Canada. I also had to coordinate correspondence between the US Pentagon and the Kenyan DOD (see copy of diplomatic accreditations in the picture section)

On the evening of Sunday, December 19, 1982, we landed at Washington-Dulles International Airport in Maryland on one of the coldest, snowiest days of the year. No one was available to pick us up because it was a weekend and most staff members were homebound due to the storm. With the heavy snowfall, only emergency vehicles and a few drivers were on the road. We took residence at the Hotel Marriott near the airport and waited for three days until offices opened after roads were cleared. After staying for about three weeks at Quality Inn in Down town Washington DC. to allow my predecessor to leave the official residence, we settled down quickly in a move-in-ready, five-bedroom government-rented home in Bethesda, Maryland. As a diplomat, the government provided transportation to work.

Since we had a nanny/house help, Mary was free and able to train as a nursing aid and get a job with the Hebrew Home of Greater Washington in Rockville, Maryland. We bought a private family car within the first month of our arrival to allow Mary transportation. We had saved a substantial amount of money paid to us as allowances for staying in the hotel while waiting for housing. Life was great for us, and within about a year, we had saved enough money to take advantage of one of our many diplomatic privileges: we ordered a customized Mercedes-Benz from Germany, making a deposit on the car, which would take another six months to custom-build. By divine unction, we ordered it in Mary's name because the family car purchase was already in my name.

JEALOUSY AND ENVY: TWIN DEMONS COME KNOCKING AT OUR DOOR

By one year and a few months into my service, faceless government officials had started focusing on me secretly and questioning the sources of my funds, comparing me with some of my counterparts who had accomplished little in years of toil at their embassy posts. What they did not know was that one day of God's favor was equal to one thousand years of human labor. What we did not know but would soon discover was that the demonic twin spirits of jealousy and envy had hounded out and caused the premature recall of progressive people serving elsewhere in foreign missions. And now they had come knocking at our door, saying, "You are next!" Little did we know that May 7, 1984, would be the last day I would report to my post, and only few minutes to return home for my suitcase and kiss my wife and children good-bye.

On that fateful morning, as I arrived for work, my boss called me into his office to deliver a well-rehearsed line, that I was needed back home for a briefing. He was getting ready to return after his term ended, which would be soon. (This part I knew.) Therefore, for the sake of continuity, I was required in Nairobi for a fresh briefing so I could effectively bridge the transition as a new boss replaced him. The first question I asked him was when I was supposed to travel to Nairobi, and without batting an eye, he told me I was to be on a plane at 6 p.m. Washington time that day. It was already past 10 a.m. A little dazed, I asked him whether I would be travelling with my family. He said no. He then released me to go home and get ready. Everything else was prepared, an air ticket and all other arrangements to convey me to the airport and from the airport on arrival.

I called my wife immediately on returning to my office and broke the news. Mary did not understand what I was trying to say, but in keeping with her character she did not express shock. All she wanted was more information because she was always a detail person. Unfortunately, information was scant. I asked her to prepare my suitcase as I had to stop on the way for a few errands related to my travel. That was all I knew at that point.

The devil in the details would be revealed slowly after I landed at Jomo Kenyatta International Airport in Nairobi on May 9 around 9 p.m. A contingent of military and civil intelligence service officers was waiting for me at the entry point. Some of the military intelligence guys were my fellow intake officers. They appeared friendly, as if they had come to ease my custom clearance. No one was allowed to say anything or to show any sign hinting that I was under restricted movement and that I was booked at the Ngong Hills Hotel on the outskirts of Nairobi. The place was to remain under heavy surveillance throughout my stay the next few nights. Unknown to me, I was considered an enemy of the state.

TREASON CHARGES READ: ENEMY OF THE STATE

My customs clearance was fast-tracked and I was quickly ferried to the hotel. Short of God's intervention, as an enemy of state I should have been taken straight to the Nyayo House, the infamous building in the heart of the city where political detainees were tortured. That was the place where many innocent Kenyans suspected of antigovernment activities had suffered for years. Some never came out alive, and most of those who survived the merciless torture were maimed and psychologically scarred for life. But God was still on His throne in heaven watching the events and listening as Mary, back in the United States, sensed in her spirit that

I was in danger and was moved to intercede, spending days and nights on her knees pleading for me from the moment I left Washington.

She later told me that this feeling hit her the moment I called her from my Washington office on that Monday morning. She sensed trouble ahead, but she remained calm and composed, not wanting to alarm me. Mary decided to fast and to pray for me while I was gone. And lo and behold, the next Monday morning when I reported to the Ulinzi House, three treason charges were waiting for me. The first was that I had plotted with top unnamed American generals based at the Pentagon, which I frequented as part of my routine duties, to topple Kenya government. Second, I was accused of belonging to the "Msaliti" network, which intended to overthrow the government (as alleged). Finally, I was charged with spreading disparaging rumors in the United States to the effect that the current government was weaker and more corrupt than the previous.

These charges were read to me by none other than the top four-star general and chief of general staff (CGS), General M. in his dreaded executive office at the Ulinzi House. No officer was ever at ease when summoned to his office even for a promotion. The major general escorting me, a two-star general, could not sit down but remained standing the whole time, quietly taking notes. But the CGS, cognizant of how nervous and frightened I might have been merely because I was in his office, graciously welcomed me to a seat directly in front of his desk. He greeted me in a fatherly tone and started by inquiring about my family. But because I had never been this close to him, much less had him address me one on one, none of his efforts made me feel much at ease.

Soon after the pleasantries, the general got down to the business of the moment, dropping the bombshells one by one. Adding to their lethality, he invoked the name of the President. He said to me that the president had called him on a hotline, asking him to find out what a Kenyan army captain named Wilfred Nkoyo, based at the Washington embassy, was up to. To me, the CGS was a proxy, the embodiment of the president, now talking to me face to face.

After he finished reading the charges, my heart literarily stopped. For a moment, I could not breathe and the whole room seemed to be filled with a red mist. I thought I was having a terrifying and cruel dream, after all I was still in a jet lag. And even when I recovered my breath and composure after what felt like an eternity in a trance, I still could not muster words to respond to the allegations. Realizing the shock I was experiencing, the CGS tried to make me comfortable by breaking the silence. He said that the source of this information was in Washington but that the matter was still under investigation. However, he did not mention where in Washington this had come from or the individuals involved.

I AM A BORN-AGAIN CHRISTIAN, NOT A POLITICIAN

When I came to, my survival instinct sprang into action. I realized that my life was in imminent danger as was the future of my family. My mind raced back to Washington DC., to my young, adoring wife and my two little children. I was oblivious to where I was headed at this moment. I believed that my next stop would be the Nyayo torture chambers. I remembered my hometown Narok, only about two hours from Nairobi, and thought I might never live to see it or my father's family again. None of my relatives had any clue that I was already in the country except my adorable mother, who had seen me return in a dream the previous night. (She shared this amazing dream with me the day I suddenly showed up at the family's doorstep in Narok, surprising everybody but her.)

Back at CGS office in Nairobi, I stood alone, facing nameless accusers and unable to say anything in self-defense or do anything to escape the lion's den awaiting me in the dreaded Nyayo House. I visualized myself in shackles with the doors to the torture chambers opening for me to join the wailing helpless souls. I resigned myself to that fate. All these thoughts raced through my mind, but when I finally opened my mouth to speak, I offered my simple testimony as a born-again Christian. I was reminded of the training seared in the mind of every POW on what to say to their captors if subjected to torture. It comes by instinct: name, rank, and service ID only. So I said to the CGS, "Sir, I am a born-again Christian, and so is Mary, my wife and closest companion. We do not indulge in matters of a political nature, and neither do our families or our fellow Christian associates. That is all I have to state sir." That statement was recorded verbatim by the only other person in the room, the chief of staff. The soft-spoken general responded, "If that is all you have to say, I will convey the same words to the president."

While I was facing the top general and hearing the most serious charges that could be leveled against a uniformed service person, my beloved wife was on her knees in the upper room of the Praise the Lord (PTL) Club in Charlotte, North Carolina. She was there while on a fast and prayer, pleading my innocence whatever the accusations were, and as if before the throne of God asking for supernatural immunity from all harm for me. That is the reason my defence had to be only a few words of testimony about me, Mary, our relatives, and our associates. This was not a rehearsed line of defence. After all, the charges had taken me by surprise. My response came purely by spiritual instinct and because Mary and I were in spiritual sync. This was the Mary to whom I owed my life. She always prevailed against our foes at my weakest moments.

From the CGS office I was made to return to the hotel with strict orders not to communicate what had transpired to anyone else until the investigations were over. I was forbidden to call my wife since I might be tempted to discuss the matter with her. In my hotel room that night, I reflected on the whole episode, the charges read to me by the chief of general staff, and how they had come directly from the commander in chief. I reviewed my simple defence, my Christian testimony concerning my wife, my relatives, and my associates, and thought the general was satisfied by that since he did not press me any further. I remembered the Scripture: "And they overcame him by the blood of the Lamb and by the word of their testimony, and they did not love their lives to the death" (Revelation 12:11 NKJV).

I did not know how things would turn out once my response was conveyed to the head of state, but my conscience was clear that my testimony was true and that I was not guilty of any of the charges. The only thing I did not know was how my wife was handling my absence and the uncertainty caused by a lack of communication. However, I was certain that this prayer warrior must have moved quickly to the front line in the spiritual realm for me and our family, which she actually did. Mary later told me what she had done from the moment I last saw her as I hurried to catch my flight to Kenya to the day she landed in Nairobi accompanied by our two beautiful children about a month and a half later.

THE PRAYER WARRIOR AT THE FRONT LINE BRACES FOR A DECISIVE BATTLE

Most remarkable is how Mary was able to sense in her spirit from the first day that something was suspicious in the way I was recalled. Though she did not raise any alarm to me, she decided to start fasting and praying. She went to her place of work later that day and asked for some days off so she could travel to Charlotte, North Carolina. She wanted to retreat for three days at the PTL ministry center. Mary was a partner in the ministry. She spent her entire time in complete fasting (no food or drink) and prayed in the upper room. While there, she asked prayer partners to join her in praying for her family and specifically for her husband, who had been recalled home abruptly under suspicious circumstances. The day I appeared before the CGS in Nairobi, Mary was on her knees in the upper room.

By the time she returned to Washington, I had been released from the hotel and instructed to go to Narok on a short compulsory leave. Meanwhile, the replacement for my boss was dispatched to Washington to further investigate the matter. During my leave and about a week after I left Washington, I decided to place a long-distance call to my wife and give her the whole story. I did this in defiance of instructions. I thought that since I had nothing to hide and had started connecting the dots concerning the sources of the fabrication, I might as well let my wife know what was happening and tell her of the uncertainties facing me both in the army and in my work in Washington.

As I write this, I feel like I am on the phone with Mary again. A patient listener, she waited until I finished the story and then said to me, "My beloved, the spirit of God revealed to me from the beginning that something had been planned against us. But as you know, no weapon formed against us shall prosper. As soon as you left, I asked for an indefinite leave from my job, left home, and took a three-day vacation to the PTL retreat center to Charlotte, North Carolina to fast and to pray, and while there, God gave me the assurance that all will be well with you and our family." Nothing in this world meant more to me at that moment than to hear Mary's confident and assured voice from more than ten thousand miles away and to know that her mind, soul, and spirit were in harmony and were focused on God's power to intervene on our behalf. My whole world lit up with hope, and joy filled my heart.

At the end of the second week, one week after our conversation, I was ordered to report to the Ulinzi House, this time to the chief of staff's office. He told me that nothing substantial had come out of the investigation in Washington by Colonel M and that the president had directed that I return to my post in Washington. However, the CGS had decided that in the interest of safety for me and my family I should not return to Washington. He was concerned that the same fabricators could come up with a more sinister plan to hurt me or my family. I was to be redeployed back to Kenya, and return arrangements for my family would be coordinated between the Ulinzi House and the Kenyan Embassy in Washington, so I would not have to worry. All I was required to do was to call my wife and ask her to put our family belongings together. Once ready, she could call the embassy for shipping arrangements.

Mary rises to the occasion as head of the family in USA

This is where Mary rose to the occasion in full force. She had two little children to mother and to father, all the family belongings, merchandise laid away in stores in several American cities, and a new custom-built Mercedes-Benz in West Germany that we had just ordered, thankfully in her name. I was concerned about how she would coordinate all this on such a short notice, and I thought to help. First I made one major suggestion. I proposed that Mary look for a private rental, maybe an apartment, and because she had a job and could afford it, that she move there. I had in the back of my mind an evolving plan to resign from the military and eventually to move back to the United States to join my family. This idea was inspired by bitterness and frustration after what I had just endured. I had already hinted to the chief of staff during our last meeting that I was going to resign.

That was the thought going through my mind as I made the suggestion to Mary, but before I could finish my proposal, she uncharacteristically ran out of patience with me. She cut me short and asked me, "Are you trying

to propose that I settle in America while my husband is in Kenya alone?"
I answered, "Yes, but only for a short time to enable me if necessary to
resign and join you."

I tried to remind her of familiar cases in which wives of diplomats
remained behind when their husbands ended their terms or were recalled—
case in point, former ambassador in Washington. But once again, before
I could finish, Mary cut me off and said, "I am not them, and it doesn't
matter whether you will continue in the army or not. All I want is for me
and our children to be wherever you will be. You are not even aware that
those who tried to dig a hole for you have approached me, trying to seduce
me, but I gave them a piece of my mind and told them who I belong to.
And right now as we talk, I have started packing because I want to leave
this country within a month."

What began as a dialogue ended as monologue. I just sat there listening
to Mary. Her heart was no longer in Washington, the capital of wealth and
glamour, but in the poverty-stricken, muddy little town of Narok where her
husband, her most valued treasure, was cornered. She finished by saying,
"Where you are is where I want to be because that is where I belong."

I changed the subject to the car in Germany. We had made a minimum
deposit, and our car was just a few months from completion, meaning
we needed to pay off the balance. Without the embassy job, it would be
almost impossible for me to afford this, and as a precaution I had foolishly
mentioned to the chief of staff my readiness to surrender the car to the
DOD. An opportunist, he had hinted that this was possible, but he must
have hoped I would sign it over to him.

The moment my wife heard my proposal to dispose of the car, she
said something I will never forget. "Go back to your chief of staff and
tell him that the car in Germany has Mary Nkoyo's name on it, and that
will not change under any circumstance. And because they prematurely
recalled you, it will be upon them to make sure all your belongings, rags
and all, wherever they may be in the world follow you to your new post or
home. Let everyone who needs to know be informed that I will not leave
the US without shipping documents in my hands for all our belongings
to the last rag wherever they may be scattered abroad. That includes all
the documents for the car in Germany showing it is fully paid for with

shipping redirected to Kenya. We also have lay-away merchandise in stores at different locations here in America. I am not leaving anything behind. They should make arrangements to deduct the total difference from your salary; after all, they recalled you abruptly before your time was up and without any good reason. The DOD should take responsibility."

Reenergized by Mary's argument and adamancy, that is the brief I took to the chief of staff when I visited the Ulinzi House for my redeployment orders. Meanwhile, back in Washington, Mary went to see the ambassador with a list of exactly what she expected in her container including all the things she had mentioned to me. This was not a request but a demand. The ambassador could not believe his eyes, wondering where in the budget that money would be found and how this stubborn little woman had the guts to look him straight in the eye and to address him without a care for the protocol and etiquette to which he had become accustomed.

Back at the Ulinzi House, the chief of staff went to consult the CGS, his boss, repeating the words of the "stubborn little woman" as nicknamed by the Kenyan defence attaché in Washington. On hearing them, the general instructed the chief of staff to grant Mary's request in full because her argument was right and to make sure she was not subjected to any undue pressure with deadlines to leave Washington or inconvenienced over packaging her family belongings. All the documents pertaining to shipments had to be given to her, and while all this was happening, my salary would be processed as if I were still in the United States because my family was still on transit. The DOD instructed the embassy in Washington to pay off outstanding balances on anything with our names on it in America or Germany, and this was to be charged against the defence section budget at the embassy.

Mary took her time, and after one month, when everything, including our Peugeot 504 station wagon, had been loaded in a forty-foot container, she was handed the bill of lading, which included documents for the car in Germany to show that it had been rerouted to Mombasa. When Mary landed at Jomo Kenyatta International Airport with our children on tow, the first things she handed me after the hugs and kisses were all the documents and the shipping container keys. This incident revealed to me a Mary I had never known. Her spiritual and moral courage, her persistence, patience, and self-confidence, her integrity, fidelity, and honesty, and her commitment to the covenant she made with me—all these came into play in Washington. I am a debtor to Mary for all I became after we met in high school. And from this act alone, she made us a millionaire family! our social status suddenly changed.

As an act of healing and damage control, I was promoted to the rank of a major in 1984, the same year I was abruptly recalled. And in line with Mary's demand, the DOD assumed all of our financial responsibilities in America and Germany, consolidated all my debts, and eventually scrubbed them from its account books. With a new vigor, I continued my military career until 1988 when I retired with a clean record of service to my country. Having served for more than twelve years, I was pensionable and am to this day. I have access to all the benefits for retired Kenyan armed forces officers.

Mary and I heard God calling us to full-time ministry, and we wanted to return to the United States where we could build it. That desire militated strongly against my continued service in uniform in spite of ever-increasing favor. Mary not only enhanced my military service, but when my life was in danger, she pulled me out of the hole where my enemies had thrown me to die. I emerged with gold and silver in my hands. This was not a work of flesh and blood, but of moral courage, impeccable decency, and unshakable faith in God in the face of hostility and uncertainties. Above all, Mary demonstrated her commitment to the covenant between us, saying, "Wherever you are is where I want to be because that is where I belong."

That was the Mary to whom I owed the whole world. I was a debtor to her for all I became. Mary made me the man of dignity I am today.

THE MERCEDES TURNS INTO A JET BACK TO THE USA

In 1992, the Mercedes-Benz that Mary's courage had secured in 1984 became the jet that would fly us back to United States of America, this time around, moving permanently to become US citizens. Before that year, I tried everything possible to sell the car, hoping to use the money for Real Estate investments. While still brand new, I had it displayed in a very strategic showroom in downtown Nairobi city for one year, but Mary, secretly waged a spiritual warfare against the idea and I could not find a buyer no matter how low I went on the price. But in the fullness of time in July 1992, soon after we secured travel visas to visit the United States, a buyer showed up.

Suddenly, we had more than enough money to pay the whole family's airfare, pay off any debts we owed before leaving Kenya, to carry the maximum foreign exchange allowed to us, and to give a large love gift to my father. All this was possible with the sale of the Mercedes that Mary's courage and boldness had forced the Kenyan Embassy in Washington and Kenya's DOD to pay off and ship to Kenya duty free in her name eight years earlier. I had attempted to sell the car several times, but Mary's faith blocked every buyer until the fullness of time when she released it in the spirit to be sold while she waited for us in the United States where she had gone ahead to prepare a place. The transaction took less than one hour, and the buyer had cash in hand. Talk of the power of prayer, talk of God's timing, talk of Spiritual sensitivity in Mary. To this day, I have kept the briefcase in which the buyer stuffed hundreds of thousands of Kenya shillings from his "Bedroom Bank." This was dramatic! It was miraculous.

CHAPTER 5

They Come to Our Home to Kill to Steal and to Destroy but find a Heavenly Host Waiting to Resist

THANKS TO MARY'S OBEDIENCE TO GOD'S VOICE

THE SABA SABA REBELLION—THE BACKGROUND

I will never forget Saturday, July 7, 1990, when my country faced a rebellion that made history. To this day it is remembered as the infamous Saba Saba, Kiswahili words meaning "the seventh of July."

Unprecedented chaos took place in Kenya on this day as a dictatorship under the Kenya African National Union (KANU) party faced civil disobedience led by a coalition of opposition groups. The enigmatic and immutable KANU had ruled for twenty-seven years from the time Kenya became independent in 1963. With time KANU became extremely corrupt and oppressive. The chaos started after the opposition held a rally at Kamukunji Stadium in Nairobi city in defiance of a government ban. The government, using crowd-dispersal police and dogs, went after the rally organizers. Resistance was strong, but the protests were eventually subdued, with many wounded in the fight.

That was Saturday. Over the following two days, there were uprisings in many other parts of the country. Chaos reigned in many urban centers. People defied the law and revolted. They vandalized private businesses, banks were robbed, and motor vehicles were set on fire by rioting mobs and other opportunists. With the government fumbling and the opposition having lost control of what was to have been a nonviolent rebellion, anarchy ensued. Thugs took advantage of the situation to violently harass and rob the unprotected public. Others decided it was time to settle scores. Anarchists and thugs targeted innocent citizens, and my family residence fell squarely in the path of their destruction.

THE ATTACK ON MY FAMILY RESIDENCE

At around midnight on July 7, an armed gang numbering about thirty descended upon my home in Limuru. In Kenya today, gangs still roam freely everywhere, attacking innocent people. They gang-rape wives and daughters, terrorize and kill members of families who try to resist, and rob them of their possessions. That must have been the gang's intention when it attacked my residence that night. Our home was located in an isolated place in the middle of a tea plantation.

In 1988, when I voluntarily retired from the army, I chose to settle in Limuru, a small farming town a few miles from Nairobi, the capital city. I planned to launch a vocational training program in the town to give opportunities to local youths. This was part of our ministry vision. The area is densely populated. Young people who cannot find places in the country's few colleges and cannot find jobs end up in gang lifestyles. We also started a hot lunch catering program through our restaurant, the Heritage Inn, delivering affordable meals on wheels to hundreds of children every school day. Our business became a household name within one year of opening. My family lived in a huge old farmhouse that we rented from a Limuru tea plantation just outside the town center where our business was located. We had no nearby neighbors (see pictures in the picture section)

We were sleeping at around eleven on that fateful night. I had become concerned about the tense atmosphere in the main shopping center where vehicles were set on fire by rampaging gangs and the chaos that followed. Though I was watching these events from a safe distance, standing outside my residence on higher ground, I was worried about my restaurant, located near the epicenter of the chaos even though we had closed early. At the end of the day, mentally exhausted, I fell into a deep sleep as soon as I lay down, but my wife lingered around the fireplace in our living room, most likely praying before finally joining me. Very soon, she was also fast asleep.

GOD MUST HAVE AWAKENED MARY

At around eleven-thirty, my wife shook me awake to tell me that our security lights had suddenly gone off. I was always the first to detect even the slightest movement no matter how deeply asleep I was, but for some divine reason, Mary, a deep sleeper was awakened this time. I shot up from the bed to find out what had happened. As soon I stepped down from the bed, I heard a commotion in the TV room, which was at the other end of the building. Our living room stood between our bedroom and the TV room. I opened our bedroom door to see what was going on in the TV room, which was separated from the living room by a glass wall.

What I saw shocked me: brilliant flashlights lit our TV room, with intruders searching everywhere. That room was where we stored all of our electronic gear, which included Band equipment and sound systems for our evangelistic ministry. We also had an expensive decked stereo and a large-screen color TV with a matching multi-system VCR set. There were many other family valuables in that room. As the gang of about ten was still trying to figure out how to start hauling the stuff out, I jumped without hesitation from my bedroom door frame, landing on the living room wooden floor, which was two steps lower. My landing caused a loud thud, and I gave a loud war cry as I ran toward the TV room, declaring death to the gang. I was dressed only in my trousers, which I had forgotten to remove in my exhaustion. However, my bold declaration, the loud stomping on the wooden floor as I ran toward them, and my war cry caused shock and awe. Yet I had not a single weapon in my hands.

The room was dark because they had cut off the lights, and so they could not figure who was with me or what I had in my hands. Judging by the sound, they guessed it was a multitude, possibly heavily armed, closing in on them fast. They had expectation that the occupants would run and hide under beds and behind sofas as people did in other homes they had burglarized. But to their surprise, this time they had picked the wrong target. This was my domain. I was an army soldier and nobody was going to violate my family's privacy rape my Mary and hurt my children or take my possessions without a fight. I made that declaration loud and clear from the beginning, telling them to prepare for total war, which would end in

51

their deaths and not mine. I spoke in their local tongue, calling them sons of perdition.

My words were bold and loud, and I spoke as I fast approached them, ready for a fight to finish. I felt like David running toward the Philistine army (1 Samuel 17:48), and these Goliaths became scared, confused, and disorganized. They lost the initiative, which I quickly I seized. They rushed out through the narrow back door, the same one they had used to break into the house. It was a pandemonium as they stumbled over each other like roaches scattering in the flip of a light switch, trying to squeeze through the opening. In fear and confusion, they fled with empty hands in the same way they had come as I followed in hot pursuit.

A supernatural energy filled every cell of my body, bolstering the natural rush of adrenaline. In addition, a mysterious blood-colored illumination, like infrared light, appeared to fill the room, and what sounded like a voice in my ears urged me to go after them like David against the Philistines. The voice gave me assurance that I was supernaturally protected against any harm. As a Christian, I knew at once that God was speaking to me, assuring me of His presence with me, and that I should not be afraid. Every time I look back at this drama, which lasted four-and-a-half hours, analyzing it scene by scene, moment by moment, I see how God protected my family and four young university students saving with us from imminent death. It was not the soldier in me who did battle, and as in the story of Jehoshaphat (2 Chronicles 20:15), the battle was not mine but the Lord's. After all, a soldier is not a superman and even less so unarmed. This was a divine coincidence between a soldier's natural courage to stand and resist and God's supernatural presence to assist.

As I got to the exit point and was about to follow after the gang, something supernatural stopped me at the smashed doorpost. I was surprised to find my Mary right behind me, pulling me back. Worried about my safety, she whispered saying, "Do not follow them outside. They must be waiting to kill you." But anger was burning like fire in every part of my being, leaving me blind and trembling. I was struggling with pride, feeling violated by thugs who had no right to enter my home and possibly to rape her first and hurt my adolescent children. But the same supernatural voice prevailed over me, saying, "Listen to your wife. Do not go past this point."

Suddenly, I realized that Mary was in the Spirit when she warned me. I stopped immediately and a calm feeling gripped me as Mary held my arm. As the thugs disappeared into the bushes around the home, I started assessing the damage to the door. I found out that a blow by the intruders had torn off the bolt. I returned to my bedroom, found a crude tool, and tried to nail the door back into place. I then figured out that the gang must have ripped off the main light fuse, which was outside, and that was why we had no electricity in the whole building. They had also cut off the phone line, and we could not call a police station—if one was still operational after the chaos. The day's chaos had disrupted law and order, and there were few if any police stations operating nearby.

As I was fixing the door, Mary rushed in the opposite direction to the bedroom at the other extreme end of the building where her four guests were crammed together in one room with mattresses on the floor. During their six days in our home, they had been fasting (absolute) and prayed in tongues without ceasing, leaving the room only to use the shower and the toilet. We had no prior contact with them until this moment. But the irony was, they were Mary's guests and not mine until this moment. I had vehemently resisted their coming, but Mary prevailed on me to let them into our home. I made no effort to converse with them or even to learn their names, until this life and death moment. I had to assign them nicknames for this operation. It was only after the attack, looking back, that I understood the divine purpose of their presence.

The four young people, whose names I heard for the first time the morning after the attack, were sent for our protection in a plan that God had put in place for our family thirty days before the incident. Members of a Christian union club from the University of Nairobi, they had felt a strong urge to go for a prayer retreat in a secluded place away from the college environment. In their search for a place that would not cost them money, they learned through our Christian friends of an open family home in Limuru where Christians retreated and prayed. They got the home phone number and called. Mary who by divine coincidence had rushed home from the restaurant at that time, picked the phone. They told her how they had discovered our home, mentioning as references, the names of ministers who had retreated there in the past.

The moment they mentioned that they wanted a place to retreat, fast, and pray, for Mary a prayer warrior, the deal was sealed, even before she could ask and take their names down, ask for further references, or their contact numbers just in case there was a change of plan. They were welcome. Later as Mary told me of the coming guests I tried to find out details, but all she knew was that they were four in number, that they belonged to the University of Nairobi Christian union, and that they would be coming in one month time. I became upset with my wife for committing herself with such flimsy details to what I called a bunch of strangers. I argued that we had just recently moved into that property and needed time to fix it before we could receive guests. (In a previous home nearby on the same farm, we used to host individuals who needed to retreat as part of our ministry.) But Mary said that because we were in ministry, we had to be ready and willing to serve God at any time with what He had provided. But no matter how she tried to spiritualize the commitment, I was not convinced that this was the right decision. I instructed her to do all she could to contact the students and cancel the offer. But my lovely and always agreeable wife, deliberately made no any such effort.

On the morning after the attack, it dawned on me how wrong I was and how fleshly driven. Mary was right, spiritually driven and sensitive to God's leading. Every time I reflect on that event, I thank God that when the students called, It is Mary and not me who picked the phone and that they never left a contact number. If they had found me, they would not have been allowed to come, and had they given Mary a contact number, I would have defiantly called them to cancel the offer. This is an example of how God takes control to force His will against our stubbornness. He cares for us and knows how easily our stubbornness can stand in the way of His perfect plans for us. In this instance, God left no opportunity for me to interfere with His plan for our protection. Scripture says, "For I know the thoughts that I think toward you, says the Lord, thoughts of peace and not of evil, to give you a future and a hope" (Jeremiah 29:11 NKJV).

THE DAY THE ANGELS ARRIVED IN HUMAN FLESH

The day the young men arrived at our doorstep they found Mary waiting. I was home, but I was still not convinced we should host them. I still felt furious inside, but the lesson awaiting me six days later, the night we were attacked, is one I will never forget until I die and reason I write about it. I had to learn to listen to the leading of the Spirit and to obey God's voice. And because God can use anybody willing to convey the message to another stubborn person, He spoke to me through Mary. However, I would engage only in a fleshly argument. But in the end, her spiritual sensitivity and obedience to God saved our family from certain death in spite of me. The young men she let into our home, whose names I never even cared to know, made all the difference. These God-sent angels in human flesh were crucial, not necessarily for what they did physically during the resistance (which was minimal), but for the mighty force they represented in the spiritual realm as described in Scripture: "So he answered, 'Do not fear, for those who are with us are more than those who are with them'" (2 Kings 6:16 NKJV).

From this experience, I also learned that the angels reported in the Bible to have appeared in human form were actually real, as in the story of Gideon: "And the Angel of the Lord appeared to him, and said to him, 'The Lord is with you, you mighty man of valor'" (Judges 6:12 NKJV). Mark that this words were spoken to a coward of the cowards! God sends His angels to our homes every day, some speaking in our languages. They come in human form without our realization. Many times they have been sent on divine missions, and yet we turn them away. Sometimes they come asking only for a cup of water, which we give reluctantly or not at all. Some are sent without knowledge of their mission. In our case, they were looking only for a place to retreat fast and pray, but the morning after the incident, God asked me to tell them that their mission was accomplished and that their ten-day fast was to end. They had their first breakfast in six days on that morning.

THE NIGHT OF TERROR: ROUND ONE

On the night we were attacked, the four young men were into their sixth day of absolute fast, no food or water. They were too weak to get involved in a fight and too young to handle the psychological trauma. (They were first- and second-year college students in Nairobi University.) When my wife told them that our home was surrounded, they were almost completely paralyzed. They appeared relieved only when my wife assured them that I had chased the intruders out of the building. She instructed them to follow her through the dark rooms and corridors to where I was. I had just finished temporarily fixing the broken door with nails. As I reached out to touch each of them in the semi-dark room, I could feel how shaken they were by the way they trembled. They had difficulty speaking in ordinary clear language. They bubbled in tongues and so loudly that anybody listening outside would have thought that a huge number of wildly animated fighters were waiting inside to kill and repulse anyone attempting to get into the building.

What amazed me throughout this time, and what I will never forget, was my Mary's courage. Mary had no prior experience of violence and had never been subjected to traumatic experience. After all, I had never used force with her or exposed her to a situation in which she had to worry about bodily harm. She had no experience of that kind in her upbringing either. That must have been why she remained composed throughout this tense situation. But certainly, Mary was firm in her faith that God was with us.

As soon as Mary brought the young men to me, the same still small voice urged me to make haste and to deploy my God-supplied troops because the gang would return soon and I should be prepared to stand and resist. The voice told me not to be afraid, for God was with us and no one would be harmed. (Recall the apostle Paul's shipwreck on the island of Melita, where according to Acts 27, he and 275 passengers with him escaped unharmed.) At that instant moment the real purpose of these four young strangers dawned on me. The voice told me not to focus on their state of shock, their physical weakness, or their fear, which was clear, but to recognize that their presence even without a single weapon in their hands was a sign of God's presence through a heavenly host. The place was already saturated with prayers that had started days prior to that moment, flowing in tongues and in their different languages. (The students were a mixture of tribes.) The young men were supernaturally armed because they were plugged into God's source of power from their days of fasting and praying and needed no human might.

As the spiritual nature of the battle became clearer, I wasted no more time worrying about how to equip my troops but instead briefed them on where to stand at the most critical windows and doors and how to make their presence known. I relied on psychological warfare tactics faking troops and weaponry. Using their presence at those critical points to suggest a large, well-distributed, and well-armed resistance teams. In a loud voice I described imaginary weapons in the hands of each of them, as I called them by assumed names since I did not know their real names. During the briefing I told them that if I walked to each of their positions and called them by the assumed name, they were to answer loudly and that if I described the weapons in their hands and their tasks, they were to acknowledge back loudly and clearly enough for the enemy outside the house to hear, even if I had to use the thugs language, (Kikuyu) which I knew.

MY DEPLOYMENT AND CONTINGENCY PLANS

I quickly decided that my defense would be limited to the stone-built portion of the house, to include—the main living room, the TV room, and the kitchen. The rest of the house had wooden walls; the doors and the windows were easy to kick in and therefore unwise and risky to try to defend. After all, my force was limited. The solid part of the building had other advantages. I had just finished reinforcing the main doors with metallic sheets on the outside and installing window grills in that part of the building. Breaking in at these points would not be a cakewalk. The only weak point in that part of the building was the small wooden door that the gang had already damaged in the initial entry, and that was where I would station myself with one of the boys.

I positioned each young man at a door or a window where I needed some presence. I also dispatched Mary, Caroline (ten), Armstrong (eight), and my niece Leah (sixteen) to the attic to remove them from a potential battle zone if the thugs managed to enter the house. I assigned one young man, Mathenge, to the attic to keep them calm and to assure their safety even though he was unarmed. I thought to myself that if we were overrun and killed, Mathenge would have the courage to make the final stand in defence of my family because he was the biggest of the four young men. But I was wrong about Mathenge as you will see later. I then took a moment to build the confidence of my unarmed force. I gave the four a quick lesson on the military concept that one man in a defence trench can resist three attackers in the open even if armed with only the crudest weapons.

As I did this, my mind flashed back to ideas my mother had shared with us when we were kids living in a small hut on the edges of a forest in our rural village. I was almost ten, and my younger brother about six years old. I was always fearful whenever my father went back to Narok town where he did carpentry work, leaving us with my mother to farm. My mother, trying to quell my obvious fears, would tell us how impossible it would be for anyone to get into our hut even after breaking down the door, how she would resist, fighting with anything at hand including pots and pans and especially the axe that she always kept under her bed.

I asked what would happen if the attacker decided to set our grass thatched roof on fire, and she said, "You would rather die resisting enemy entry into your house than hope for mercy after he has gained entry. The only exception to this rule is when the attacker decides to set the house on fire because you have no choice but come out and face your enemy in the open, but even then, you still have an advantage over your attacker: the element of surprise. If you must emerge, you must do so violently, going straight after your attacker and not running away from him. Go for the leader, the biggest first because more often than not if you disabled the leader, leaderless followers run for their lives. Evil people are always cowardly and fearful of death." My "general" and hero would then conclude by sharpening her axe one more time and showing us where she would stand and how she would act in the event. You could never doubt my mother's toughness, she lived through the famous Mau Mau terror.

My mother's concept was reinforced by my training in artillery and infantry warfare. Only white phosphorous-loaded bombs, which rain down a burning chemical substance, would force dug-in infantry troops to abandon their trenches, and when they come out, they must emerge with their guns blazing and their bayonets fixed, ready for slaughter. So my mother was right: a defender inside a house had advantages over an attacker and should be ready to die resisting rather than surrender with the hope of begging for mercy from the intruder. All these thoughts passed through my mind as I prepared myself and my God-sent force to take their position, to stand and to resist.

I was certain that after having walked out of the gold mine empty handed, the intruders were motivated to return.

Everything my mother and the army taught me came in handy when the thugs returned exactly about a half-hour since I chased them away. They demolished every door and window in the abandoned parts of the building, picking every valuable they could find before turning their energy to where we were, and after several hours of repulsed attempts they threatened to set the house on fire if I continued to deny them entry. But I dared them to do it and swore to kill these thugs even if I had to die with the last of them.

DETAILS OF THE RESISTANCE – NIGHT OF TERROR ROUND TWO

With my troops well deployed and briefed, I took my position at the weakest point, the spot where the gang had come through the first time. The thin wooden door was barely hanging on its hinges. With the bolt lock gone, it was now held in place by two little nails. I paired myself with the smallest young man, Rukenya. He was about 120 pounds at most and about five feet tall, but he proved to be the best warrior among the lot. He was determined to fight and die side by side with me if it came to that. That testimony brought tears to my eyes, and I still feel tears flooding my eyes when I recall the rest of his confession the morning after.

When the gang returned in their round two, my wife was looking through the attic window, and she could not believe what she saw: a large crowd was emerging from the edge of the tea plantation behind our home and advancing toward our home. Though the moon was unusually bright, I had not seen the mob because of my lower elevation on the ground floor.

My wife and my niece screamed at the top of their voices, hoping to attract help from neighbors. Unfortunately, we had not even one close neighbor, as the enemy well knew. Perhaps Mary, who was also aware of that fact, hoped against hope to scare the attackers, but they kept advancing.

Caroline and Armstrong had fallen asleep soon after the first round, unconcerned about the looming danger. Mary their heroic mother, had led them in prayer and a confession of Gods assured protection. She assured the children that all would be well with God's help. In fact, before Caroline finally fell asleep, she professed her faith in God, saying, "I am not worried about those guys because I know God will protect us." The screaming and the hours of commotion didn't disrupt their sleep, but the following morning they woke up to the mess of a partially demolished home and a bloody wound on their father's eyebrows.

Alerted by Mary's scream, I looked outside through the window. By now the mob had closed in, and with the help of the bright moonlight, I estimated that close to thirty individuals were advancing in an extended formation. They covered the entire length of the building from the backyard, about 120 feet. They appeared to have objects in their hands as they advanced toward the back wall. At that moment and in response to the scream, the well-coordinated gang released a salvo of huge stones, which landed on most of the rear windows and on the wall of the long building, including the attic, shattering all the glass windows almost at once. Fortunately, the windows in the part of the building where we were holed up had recently been reinforced with metal grills, and despite the shattered glass, we were still safe inside.

With that opening salvo, my adrenaline suddenly shot up. I became highly animated and wild. I was now more than ever ready for battle and for a fierce resistance to death from my chosen position. I knew that this spot would be the thugs' first objective because that is where they had seen the treasure of electronic goods. The still small voice said, "Be strong and of good courage. I am with you. Resist them. I will give you victory." This brought to memory a similar Scripture verse: "You will not need to fight in this battle. Position yourselves, stand still and see the salvation of the Lord, who is with you ... Do not fear or be dismayed ... go out against them, for the Lord is with you" (2 Chronicles 20:17 NKJV).

I also remembered my mother saying, "You should never be afraid of people attacking you from outside the house, regardless of their number." Her dramatization with an axe, chopping off heads of intruders came alive. That scene kept replaying in my mind, and I could not imagine how the thugs could get into my stronghold even if they were to break the doors. I simply would not let them as long as I was standing on my feet, even without a weapon in my hands.

The shattered windows made it easier for me to hear and to be heard by the thugs as I dared them to enter. They also heard me calling out the given names of the young men and giving orders on what to do if anyone tried to get past their positions. I called out to my wife and my niece, who were still screaming for help from neighbors. I shouted loudly enough so the attackers could hear what I said: "You need to be quiet, ladies. We don't need any help from neighbors, because we have enough force and weaponry to handle the situation. Do not call for help. We can handle it." I spoke in the thugs' language so they could understand.

I then called out names of my boys, describing the fictitious weapons in their hands, and as they responded one by one, I told them, "Hear me! Hear me! There will be no move from your positions at the windows and the doors. You must fight with aim to kill intruders. You have clear orders from me to use your axes and your machetes to chop the heads, the legs, and the arms of any person who dares come through your positions. The heads of these sons of perdition must roll. They came to die and we must kill each of them." I made sure that the gang heard it all in their Kikuyu language, and because the students were from different tribes, I repeated this instruction in English.

Next I addressed the gang members. By this time they were busy demolishing the house. They had come with all kinds of weaponry short of firearms. They had spears, sledgehammers, hoes, machetes, clubs, huge rocks, and wooden logs each carried by four people. They would swing a log at a door or a window grill, bringing it down with the whole frame.

As they focused their energy on our stronghold, where we were holed up, I welcomed them promising total war and death. I made it clear to them that I was a professional soldier of the Kenya army and for that matter a commander of fighters ready to fight from inside and outside and to die with the last thug. I said, "Make no mistake, crazy sons of the Devil. The man you are challenging to a fight is a well-seasoned, trained, and tested Kenyan army officer and soldier. He is trained and has trained others to kill and not to be killed, but if he must die today, he will die with honor and only with the last of you. You know that I owe nothing to any of you. This house is not your property. Neither is it on your land. You all came today for one thing, and I assure you that you will get it. You came to die! Death is all I owe you, and I promise to pay." I spoke in their Kikuyu language so they that would get the message clearly.

They heard the message but continued their rampage, going back and forth, knocking down more doors and windows on each part, the wooden (undefended) and the stone (defended) parts. Meanwhile, the Lord spoke to me in the clearest voice, saying, "Put all your trust in me. Do not be afraid or give up. Resist them and I will save you and your household."

By around 2 a.m., most of the doors and windows in the unoccupied rooms had been knocked down and parts of the wooden walls torn. The thugs had ransacked all the vacant bedrooms, but in their minds they had yet to reach the goal, the gold mine, treasure they had managed only to behold with their eyes the first time they broke into the house but couldn't seize. The vivid images, still fresh in their minds, were alluring, and that was one reason they had to return and were prepared not only to demolish the house but to kill the occupants to access it.

But so far getting to the treasure was proving a mission impossible. Even though they had shattered all the glass windows and shaken loose some grills around the gold mine, resistance inside remained fierce. Though we were unarmed, I made sure that every rock or other object thrown at us through any opening went right back out, landing squarely on their faces. They could not see their targets inside the darkened rooms, but I could see them clearly under the brilliant moonlight. Meanwhile, I paced the floor back and forth to pick up the objects as soon as they landed and hurled them at the attackers but my angels stood still in their position maintaining a presence and with loud prayers in tongues.

INCHING CLOSER AND CLOSER TO THE CLIFF EDGE

Earlier on, just before abandoning our master bedroom and tightly bolting the door leading to it, I remembered to bring out some arrows and a bow that I had kept under my bed. They belonged to my watchman, who had gone home for what he said was a short leave. (After the incident, Mary and I suspected that he could have been part of the gang, an insider who had all the information about our home. One fact pointing to that possibility was that he never returned even to pick up his belongings following the attack.) I had carried the items to the living room, hoping to use them if the gang returned. At around 2:30 a.m., as the fight intensified, I remembered the arrows, which were now stashed in one corner of the defended room. Our main stronghold was about to be overrun after hours of pounding the metal grills. We were surrounded on every side. With many of the grills shaking and about to fall down, only the unarmed young men would soon be standing in the way of the determined gang. I kept calling out and encouraging them to be ready to strike hard if anybody attempted to sneak in through their positions. (Keep in mind that the young men had no weapons and were scared to death.) We were inching closer and closer to the precipice, but the still small voice persistently cheered me on, "Do not give up. Do not be afraid. Hold on to the promise. I will save you, your family, and friends."

THE ARROW THAT WOULD TURN THE TIDE AGAINST THE "GOLIATH"

Since the beginning of the fight, my main weapon had been the rocks the thugs hurled at us. I would feel for them in the darkness, pick them up, and hurl them right back. Things got far more precarious when a double-wide window grill was about to fall from the wall. It was directly opposite where I was busy engaged with about six men determined to come through the flimsy wooden door. The anchors on the window grill were barely holding onto the wall. Here, I had positioned a young man named Otieno who was unfamiliar with such violence and was the most scared of the lot. The window glass had already been completely shattered. The gang was working hard on the stubborn grill, which would not go down easy. The thugs hit it repeatedly with a log, and it was just about to drop from the wall.

Otieno was paralyzed by fear as he saw himself face to face with death. He and the others could only rattle in tongues, their only weapon, pleading in unison for God's intervention. His position was about twenty feet from where Rukenya and I were blocking the most critical spot, the wooden door. We were battling about six determined thugs who were trying to enter through into the TV room, the ultimate goal.

The flimsy wooden door at that entry had been chopped to pieces and the remaining bottom half knocked of the frame (see pictures at the picture section). The china cabinet (flipped on its side) that we used to block the entrance became the only barrier between us and the gang. However, the cabinet, only half the door's height, blocked the entrance only halfway up (see picture). The open space at the top allowed the gang to hurl rocks at us, one of which hit me on the forehead, cutting deep into my right eyebrow. The blood that gushed out momentarily blinded my eyes. Initially, I thought I had lost my right eye, but the moment I wiped off the blood and realized that I could still see, my morale shot up. Thank God there was no lull in the resistance.

The thugs made every effort to break down the cabinet, bringing in a heavy-duty log. Four men swung it in unison and hit the cabinet hard enough to push it several feet from the entrance. The young man and I slammed it back onto the doorway. This exchange was repeated several times. At the same time, I kept the attackers engaged by hurling back the rocks they threw over the open space above the cabinet, hitting their heads hard. But it was only by God's miracle that we held this position, denying the determined gang entry through this weakest point.

I saw what looked like a bloodstained curtain that appeared between us and the attackers, covering the opening above the cabinet. The mysterious curtain appeared to block the entrance every time the gang hit the cabinet, pushing it back several feet and leaving the opening free. It also concealed us from the thugs. I could see them, but they could hardly see us. This mystery later reminded me of the story of the prophet Elisha and the siege at Dothan (2 Kings 6:8–23). The divine protection was real and visible. God's wall of protection was all around us even where it was not as obvious as in this particularly critical spot. The rooms were filled with a bloodstained mist through which we could see our attackers but they could not see us. We were supernaturally concealed from the enemy. It was phenomenal.

Stealthily so the gang at the critical spot would not know that I was leaving Rukenya alone, I decided to go and reinforce Otieno. His position was now about to fall. At that moment, the still small voice brought to my memory the arrows I had stashed in the dark corner. This was timely because I might have wasted the arrows on less important targets in a less critical phase of the resistance, which had continued relentlessly for almost four hours. I rushed to the corner, and feeling my way, I grabbed them. Now, armed with five arrows in my hands, I rushed back to my partner and whispered to him, "I have to go back to that window and help Otieno, but you must keep the cabinet in place at any cost to deny these thugs entrance. Use all your might to keep this entrance blocked if you want to remain alive! I will be back."

I tiptoed to Otieno. By that time, about five guys were clustered together, getting ready to jump in one by one as soon as the precariously hanging grill fell. I took a position at one corner of the shattered window, mounted my first arrow, and tugged it to the maximum tension that I could muster while aiming at the human cluster around chest level. Remember that while I could see them clearly, the bloodstained mist concealed me from their view. I released the arrow at point-blank range, and suddenly, suddenly a very loud scream of pain was heard all around the compound. It was almost as loud as Mary and Leah's screams for help, but this time around, it was the enemy's turn to scream for help. A commotion ensued, reminding me of the pandemonium when I chased the thugs out through the narrow door the first time.

One of them had been fatally shot, and he cried and wailed in pain, saying in Kikuyu, "Wooi niaraturatha!" or "Oh! He is shooting at us." The crowd dispersed quickly from that window which by now was a ready open entrance with the grill barely hanging on loose anchors. But after that fatal arrow shot, no one would dare go back there. Word of the shooting must have spread quickly through the gang because the groups crowding other weakened windows dispersed quickly.

I rushed back to my spot. Thank God that Rukenya was still hanging in there for dear life, but of course the supernatural curtain was in place. I mounted my second arrow and aimed at the cluster pounding on the cabinet. Luckily for them, the arrow passed between two of the attackers, narrowly missing the head of one of them. It hit the stone wall behind them, causing sparks, and then it ricocheted and fell at their feet, broken in many pieces.

This arrow had the same psychological impact as the first. The multi-barbed blade, six inches long by one inch wide, must have embedded itself deep in the chest of the first thug at the window, maybe tearing into the heart, the lungs, or other vital organs. Embedded arrows are very hard to retrieve; highly risky surgery is required. Such a blade embedded in the chest, especially in the rib cage, would be impossible to remove, and victims of arrow shots are more likely to die from their wounds that are victims of bullet shots. The thugs dispersed and regrouped to discuss setting our home on fire and burning my family alive as a final act of revenge. This was the only option left to punish me for resisting them and fatally wounding one of their comrades.

By this time, around 4:30 a.m., they had destroyed twenty-one windows and eight doors and torn off part of the roof but had not gained access to their main targeted area. The lure of the gold mine was still strong despite their first casualty.

THE GANG ANNOUNCES PLANS TO SET OUR HOME ON FIRE

At around 5 a.m., the thugs announced that since I had stubbornly resisted them and had fatally wounded one of their own, they had decided to burn down the house. They had sent for gasoline to carry out their plan. They gave me a choice: let them in to do what they had come to do or die in a burning house with my family. For a moment I was scared for my wife, my children, and my guests. I imagined my family and the innocent young men burning alive. I wondered if surrender wouldn't be a wise choice and whether that would help me protect them. A strange voice said to me, "Don't be foolish. Give up. Otherwise you will die and cause the destruction of the family you are trying to protect. What will you gain?" But immediately a still small voice countered, saying, "I promised to protect you and your household. Do not be afraid. That is a devil's lie. They won't burn down the house. They have no gasoline. I want you to talk tough to them. Do not negotiate with them or beg for mercy. Do not let them in. Resist them!"

From the still small voice, I got a new surge of courage and boldness, and I replied defiantly, saying, "You evil, bunch of cowardly men, decide for yourselves what you want to do. If you decide to burn this house down, you may do so, but be sure of this one thing. By the time the roof comes down, I will be out there contending with you in a fierce fight, and if I must die, I will die with the last of you cowards. I am a soldier." These words I spoke in Kikuyu, their language. On hearing that, they responded, "Kirimu giki ugukua tuhu?" This translates as "You fool. Are you willing to die for nothing?"

Suddenly I heard a vehicle movement. They had managed to obtain the key to our Mercedes-Benz from our abandoned bedroom, which they had ransacked along with other rooms. They removed the car from the garage and used it to ferry the loot from our house to a collecting point away from our compound. They made several trips. When they returned from the first trip, I thought they must have brought the gas to set the house on fire, and fear for my family haunted me again. In a dramatic move, Mathenge, whom I had sent to the attic to keep my family calm, came downstairs in a hurry and pleaded with me in whispers to let the thugs in rather than let them burn us alive. That angered me as it stirred my fears afresh that I was risking many lives including those of our guests, but the same still voice intervened immediately, countering my fears by using the same words of assurance.

Immediately, I ordered Mathenge back to his post in the attic and told him that surrender was not an option. He complied. In fact, the vehicle had returned without any petrol. The gang was using it simply to ferry stolen goods from our house. I know in my heart that the thugs did not just decide to change their plan to burn us all alive. They had every reason and means to do so, but God must have caused confusion among them, forcing them to abandon the plan. They came up with yet another creative plan: to descend upon the gold mine from the roof since they could not enter through the broken windows without the risk of being shot with arrows. Members of the gang found their way onto the roof and started removing the tiles. They announced that since I had resisted them from the ground, they would descend on me from above.

The thought that the very family I was trying to protect would have to contend with the thugs upstairs while I was engaged with the rest of the mob downstairs frightened me more than anything else. I could imagine the thugs raping my wife, my niece, and my daughter, and killing them. The thought was nerve-racking, and I could not handle it. After all, Mathenge, whom I had assigned to keep them calm and to protect them, would not have been a match for the thugs. He is the same young man who had earlier left his post and tried to persuade me to give up the resistance.

As I was pondering this and seeking wisdom deep down inside, the still small voice repeated the same words, and suddenly a spirit of courage and defiance surged inside me, inspiring words that I spoke in Kikuyu. I said, "Kana mugukunuka kuma nathi ta makunu, kana mukugua kuma naiguru ta mbura ya mbembe, muthiaini wa uhoro, ngumurenga mitwe, kana maguru. Mukite gukua na ninii ngumuraga macaitani maya. Nii ndikua na wanyu wa muthia!" This translates as "Whether you are going to pop up from the ground like mushrooms or drop from the skies like hailstones, the end of the story is same. I will chop off your heads or chop off your legs. You came here to die, and it is my duty to kill you devils. I will die with the last of you."

Those words, supernaturally inspired, sent a chilling fear into the men who were busy tearing up the roof. They abandoned the plan and soon descended. That would become the last action in the whole drama. The operation was over after four-and-a-half hours of intense and relentless engagement meant to drain me physically and to wear out my will to resist. But as God increased my strength and inspired my will to resist with passing time, their resources were decreasing at the same rate. By 6 a.m. they ran out of steam and it was time to leave with their dead, their wounded and worthless clothing and fabrics they had taken from our rooms. The only expensive item in their hands was our Mercedes-Benz, but God would not let them get far with it or damage it in any way! I believe with all my heart, that God preserved our Benz because in two years' time (August 1992), he would be converting it into a "Jet" to fly us out to USA.

A HEAVY TRAIL OF BLOOD TO A POSSIBLE DEATH

The arrow wound to the gang member must have been fatal, judging by a heavy trail of blood that marked the thugs' exit route. We followed this trail the following morning, picking up family photographs and documents, including Mary's passport (with a current US visa that she would need two years later) strewn along the tracks that ran through tea plantations. If the victim died on the way, the gang members might have dumped his body in a trench to cover their tracks and hide their identities.

In a fight that started around midnight and continued relentlessly until 6:00 a.m., we saw God build a shield of protection around us, super-energizing me in the physical sense and our God-sent angels in the spiritual. In the end, He gave us victory in the face of a determined, better-equipped, and much superior force. Through His still small voice, He brought words of assurance and promise to keep us from harm, urging me to trust Him, to refuse to be intimidated by threats or numbers, and to be courageous, talking and acting tough to the end. God kept the promises He made in Scripture: "'No weapon formed against you shall prosper, and every tongue which rises against you in judgment you shall condemn. This is the heritage of the servants of the Lord, and their righteousness is from Me,' says the Lord" (Isaiah 54:17 NKJV).

A MORNING OF REFLECTION

After the gang had finally left the compound and all was quiet, we made a big bonfire in the fireplace in the living room, the bloody battleground where we had resisted the thugs for almost half of the night. The morning was cold and misty. The windows had all been shattered, and the window grills were barely anchored. One of the doors had been completely chopped up. The morning air was streaming through, making the room extremely cold despite the fire. My face was swollen with a deep open wound on the right eyebrow. The soles of my bare feet were swollen and embedded with broken glass. I could hardly stand or walk due to the pain. The carpet had huge bloodstains from my soles and my face.

But despite the destruction of property; the losses, including our precious Mercedes-Benz; the pain from wounds; the aching in every part of my body, and the extreme physical and mental fatigue, my heart was filled with joy and praise unto God for His faithfulness in keeping my family safe and for the human angels He sent to watch over us. (They did not have to fight physically, but they waged war in the spiritual realm.) As my wife and my children gathered around me unharmed and with smiles on their faces, my heart was filled with eternal gratitude to God. Throughout an ordeal that filled every cell in my body with fear and uncertainty, God's supernatural courage and words of assurance made me rise above all my doubts and human limitations. At no point did God leave me alone to figure out what to do. Instead He guided me step by step, going ahead of me. He ensured that every flank was covered by His angels. That included the roof, which according to the enemy was an open flank.

Lessons learned—hearing and obeying God

Of the many lessons I drew from this experience, one stands starkly above the rest: we must be sensitive to God's still small voice and obedient in following His lead. My beloved wife Mary had over the years developed a sharp spiritual ear. Thus she moved in obedience and opened doors to our home for protective Angels way in advance. She was perfectly in accord with God's Word: "Let brotherly love continue. Do not forget to entertain strangers, for by so doing some have unwittingly entertained angels" (Hebrews 13:1–2 NKJV).

With her spiritual sensitivity, Mary could hear God's still small voice even in her deepest sleep. While we were both soundly asleep, she woke me up as soon as the enemy cut off our electricity in preparation for breaking into our home and surprising us asleep in our bedroom. When I nearly followed blindly into the enemy's trap outside the door, she pulled me back, warning me that the attackers were waiting to kill me. In the midst of chaos and confusion, she remained calm, walked all the way through darkness to the room she had prepared for our angels, and led them through the dark corridors to safety in the strong room where I was able to deploy them. She was always confident that God would protect us even in this most desperate situation. That is why she did not panic and run to the nearest place where she could hide but remained alert and calm throughout and assured our children that God was in control and that He would keep them safe in their sleep.

This is the Mary to whom I was always indebted. Whether up in health or down sick and in the gutters of depression, until the time she lay still in that casket, Mary was the queen of my life.

SCARY CONFESSIONS FROM THE HUMAN SIDE OF ANGELS

As we sat around the fireplace the morning after the terror, Rukenya, the only angel who participated physically throughout the operation, made a shocking revelation. He was with me at the weakest and most critical position in the building. There was no barrier besides the small china cabinet we held against the broken door. To my astonishment, he confessed to us that the moment the little wooden door was completely destroyed and the only thing left to block the entrance was the cabinet, he briefly considered letting go of the cabinet, crawling off, and hiding under a nearby couch to save his life. Judging by his body size, Rukenya could have fit in a small cleft and maybe saved himself. He reasoned that when the cabinet broke up, he would be the first to die as a punishment for resisting and wearing out the attackers.

However, he said, "As I was down on one knee with my hands pressing on the cabinet against the opening, I looked up and I could see your face in the faint moonlight coming through the open space above the cabinet. I could see clearly how hard you were fighting and determined to continue the resistance. But I noticed something else so unique, a supernatural glow emanating from your face in the darkness, a supernatural courage, and such a determination to keep up the fight. And from that moment, I decided in my heart that if this resistance was to end with death, then I would rather die side by side with you than to abandon you in a bid to save myself."

This testimony shocked me as I tried to imagine what would have happened if the young man had abandoned his position the time I left him alone to attend to other imminent break-ins, especially when I went to reinforce Otieno as his position was about to fall. This was a defining moment in the resistance, the place I shot one of the thugs and turned the tide against our enemy. If the young man had given in to temptation and let go of the cabinet, the thugs would have marched in with fury. I would have been forced to turn around, and my plan to reinforce Otieno's position would have been disrupted. In that case, two positions would have fallen at the same time, and we would have been overrun from multiple directions and perished!

This was just when God was about to give us the most powerful final blow into the heart of the enemy thus breaking the enemy's back and bring us a decisive victory. The enemy would have overrun and killed us all because one person almost believed the Devil's lie that he could save his own life even if he put the rest of us at risk. There are many people who, faced with life's challenges, give up when victory is just around the corner! This drama taught me lessons that came in handy when I was dealing with the health challenges that faced my hero Mary, especially in her last five years of life as she struggled with depression and kidney failure at the same time.

If you don't give up in life's challenges but trust God, He will raise His banner, a symbol of victory over your circumstances. According to Scripture, "When the enemy comes in like a flood, the Spirit of the Lord will lift up a standard against him" (Isaiah 59:7 NKJV). God honored courage, the soldier in me, and my late model mother who told me never to surrender or give in to an enemy, no matter how strong.

THE SPIRITUAL SYMBOLISM AND RELEVANCE

The urge to prayer and fasting in the four young people at our place at that time was the provision God made to save my family during a chaotic situation He had foreseen. Remember, this was the fifth day and the sixth night of absolute fasting by the four young men. They had not eaten or drunk anything. They had spent all their time in a secluded room in our house praying around the clock. When the tragedy struck, they were not only frail and frightened, but the shocking experience drained the little energy left in their starved bodies. They also paid a price for being there for us in that most of their belongings were stolen when their room was ransacked. Their clothes and shoes were among the first things to go, and during the long night they were down to their pajamas.

That morning as we sat by the fireplace, I looked at their hollow eyes and noticed how their bodies were shaking due to the cold and the trauma. The Lord spoke to me and told me to declare their mission over and that they were to immediately break the fast. I was to tell them that they had been on a special mission to provide a divine shield to protect us from harm but that their physical might had no role to play because God wanted to demonstrate His power through weakness. Their assignment was simply to take the positions I assigned to them. Because God is a spirit, He operates through physical beings sanctified unto Him. The purpose of their ceaseless and fervent prayers in an absolute fast was to sanctify themselves, starting five (number for God's Grace) days prior to the operation. Their dynamic prayers throughout the night of terror linked the earthly battleground to the heavenly source of supernatural power, as Moses had done on the mountain.

Tapping into that power, my role was to be Joshua fighting physically the Amalekites in the valley of Rephidim. According to Scripture, "Moses said to Joshua, 'Choose us some men and go out, fight with Amalek. Tomorrow I will stand on the top of the hill with the rod of God in my hand'" (Exodus 17:9 NKJV).

Mary's role was clearly that of faithful Aaron and Hur, who supported Moses to ensure he was in position on the mountain and propped up to pray. Thirty days prior to the night of terror, Mary welcomed the four young students to our home. Before the day they arrived, she set aside a special room (mountain) at their request and as a prayer warrior herself, made sure that they had everything they needed to ensure they could pray in comfort. That is obedience. "But Moses' hands became heavy; so they took a stone and put it under him, and he sat on it. And Aaron and Hur supported his hands, one on one side, and the other on the other side; and his hands were steady until the going down of the sun. So Joshua defeated Amalek and his people with the edge of the sword" (Exodus 17:12–13 NKJV).

With these words, I asked the young men to break their fast and to have their first breakfast in six days with us. Their mission of ten days had been accomplished in six. We clothed those who had lost most of their belongings, and soon they were on their way back to the University of Nairobi campus where they told of God's greatness with a story they have repeated over and over to this day.

That is the reason we are alive today as a family. Otherwise we would have perished in Limuru, Kenya, in 1990, murdered in cold blood or burned alive with no trace but ashes left behind. "Then the Lord said to Moses, 'Write this for a memorial in the book and recount it in the hearing of Joshua'" (Exodus 17:14 NKJV).

My purpose in telling this story and in writing this book is to honour God. His mighty hand delivered my family when we were surrounded by a bloodthirsty mob on a mission to steal, to kill, and to destroy us. But using His obedient servant Mary, God saved us. I am forever indebted to her faithfulness and grateful to God for giving her to me as a wife, counselor, priest, and best friend; an exemplary mother to my children, the grandmother of my grandchildren, and a model matriarch for future Nkoyo generations.

PART 3

New Opportunities New Challenges (1992–2009)

CHAPTER 6

By Faith Mary Pursues Our Preordained Inheritance

In retrospect, I can testify to the fact that every good, bad, and ugly thing that took place in our lives as a family in the first eighteen years after Mary and I met in high school worked together for our good in the end and in line with God's preordained plan to bring us out of Kenya, our motherland, and into another country of inheritance, giving us a fresh new beginning. Scripture tells us how Abraham was called by God out of his country. "Now the Lord had said to Abram: 'Get out of your country, from your family and from your father's house, to a land that I will show you'" (Genesis 12:1 NKJV). Abraham took his wife Sarai with him. Likewise in obedience to God, I got out of Kenya my country in 1992 with my wife Mary and our children, Caroline and Armstrong to the United States of America. And from the day we landed, God's provisions started to flow and to this day I am writing we have never lacked anything, even for one day.

GOD ORDERS OUR STEPS—NEVER SETTLE FOR LESS BUT GOD'S BEST

In 1988 I retired from the army, but instead of going straight back to my hometown Narok, I took my family and settled in an entirely new place called Limuru in the Kiambu district of Kenya. It was a costly detour because I had made huge investments in Narok, but I was not keen to resettle in what I considered a socially and politically polluted environment. In Limuru, we started a new life and a catering business. We prospered to the envy of many older local business people, leading to the invasion of our home on the *Saba Saba* night. Our vision was to expand our meals-on-wheels business to schools beyond the area, but God's plan for us would not crystalize in such comfort. It took only one night of terror to bring our catering business to a full stop, and we were on the move in a hurry.

I reluctantly took my family to Narok, hoping to start afresh, but here nothing seemed to work except a Laundromat business, the first of its kind in town. In 1991, following the death of my mother and hero, the best friend to my wife Mary and an adored grandmother to our children, nothing was of value to us in Narok anymore. We did not want to deal with the invasive politics of Narok or the corrupt system that was unprepared for change.

We needed a way out and the only place we could think of was the United States of America the land of the free. That was the only other environment we had tested, and found suitable. This happened during my service as assistant defense attaché at the Kenyan Embassy in Washington from 1982 to 1984. God had a divine purpose from the beginning for giving me that appointment out of many other candidates. This was His divine favor.

During that short period, we prayed and believed in the Scripture, which says, "Every place that the sole of your foot will tread upon I have given you, as I said to Moses" (Joshua 1:3 NKJV). But the fashion in which we were plucked out of the United States in May 1984, before the end of my term, had indicated otherwise. Only years later did I discover that the circumstances fabricated to destroy me would become our ***reason*** to return to America, including the return ***airfare,*** eight years later (number for new beginning) this time not on a tour of duty or as visitors, but as citizens and inheritors of the greatest and most powerful nation on earth.

All things, the good, the bad, and the ugly, worked together for our good, paving our way to a land coveted by millions, if not billions, around the globe. According to scripture: "And we know that all things work together for good to those who love God, to those who are the called according to His purpose" (Romans 8:28 NKJV).

And this is how our journey of miracle after miracle began.

MARY SUGGESTS A RETREAT TO SEEK GOD'S WILL FOR OUR NEXT MOVE

After realizing that nothing seemed to be working in Narok, we decided to take our children away to another district and to put them in a boarding school so Mary and I could have more room to reconfigure our future. We decided to enroll them in Kaptagat Preparatory School in Eldoret, a competitive school managed by one of our best Christian friends, Samuel Gachengechi, and his beautiful wife Judy. That was at the beginning of 1992. On our way back from Eldoret, we decided to stop at the American Embassy in Nairobi to see whether Mary could get a visa to the United States. It was about our third attempt, but unfortunately once again it was denied. We returned to Narok disappointed.

On our way back, we had discussed the need to seek fresh direction from God on the future, and Mary had suggested that now the children were gone, we could make a short retreat where we could fast and pray for that direction. However, we did not decide on a venue. As we approached town Narok, depression gripped us, with bad memories of a hostile social-political environment and projects that we had tried to do without much success. I suddenly remembered the words of desperation that came from my wife's lips in one of those moments of despair in that town: "Riu nii nyina wa Ciku ngwika atia?" This Kikuyu vernacular expression means "Now what shall I, mother of Ciku, do?" These words were not directed at me and were not intended for my hearing or response. They were spoken by an overwhelmed person who had reached a dead end, but by spiritual instinct, Mary was looking up from where her help came.

Nevertheless, I became alarmed, interpreting this as a sign of desperation, because Mary was the last person to reach such a point. Later I decided that maybe this was the time to do what she had suggested earlier and go for a short retreat. Something she had done before when she went missing temporarily years earlier from this same town. I proposed that we pack a bedroll in the trunk of our Mercedes-Benz and head out to a remote area called Maji Moto and there retreat in a rural church that I knew was vacant most weekdays and whose doors were never locked. It was located thirty to forty miles from Narok and belonged to our denomination, the Pentecostal Assemblies of God. Having taken nothing for food or drink, we could fast and pray day and night uninterrupted. Mary agreed and soon, like the hillbillies we were in our youth, when we used to preach in the country sides with little preparation, we hit the road to Maji Moto.

After our retreat, we decided to go straight to Nairobi, bypassing Narok on our way, to test our faith. This time it was my turn to try the British Embassy to see if I could get a visa to the UK. We believed that if we could get one foot outside of Kenya, the other would follow. But here again we hit a rock, and I was denied. Still aglow with the anointing from our retreat, Mary suggested we visit the family of Peter Karanja (Kijana Wa Yesu), a Christian friend whom we had not seen in a long time. He and wife lived on the outskirts of Nairobi in a place called Banana Hills. Lo and behold, that is exactly where God wanted us to be for the night so He could point out a door to the United States, a door that He had opened almost five years prior but that had been concealed from us until that moment. That night would mark the beginning of our relocation journey to America with Mary as the pioneer to our preordained land of inheritance.

We had a wonderful reunion and fellowship with the Karanjas, talking till almost midnight before we shared the purpose of our visit to Nairobi that day. As we discussed the reluctance of embassies to issue visas, brother Karanja asked Mary if he could see her passport to compare the number of denial rubber stamps with those in his passport, as they were numerous. As he turned the pages of Mary's passport, he came across a five-year, multiple-entry B-1/B-2 US immigration visa in her passport issued on June 2, 1987, which was still current but due to expire on June 1, 1992. We were almost at the end of March 1992. The visa had only two months remaining before expiration. But because Mary happened to have been issued an F-1 student visa soon after that in 1987 and it had expired in 1988 before she could use it, we had always assumed that it had automatically cancelled the previous visa.

This is where Karanjas knowledge of how visas worked became handy. Comically as always, brother Karanja started screaming at the top of his voice, asking why we had been bothering the US Embassy when Mary had a current visa. We were skeptical and thought he was pulling our legs, but as he explained how visas worked, we became convinced. The following day early in the morning, we got Mary an air ticket to the United States, and in less than two weeks on March 29, 1992, she walked through the immigration entry gates into New York.

Mary hit the ground running, travelling and ministering among churches and groups, meanwhile praying and fasting for many days on end that God would open the doors for her family to join her. God opened door after door for her to minister, but months would follow before a door for us to join her finally opened. All this time we were in communication regularly, and I had established a prayer vigil group in our home in Narok to back her up. By the fifth month, Mary started wearing out. She had never been away from her family that long, and she got lonely and asked if she could return. I persuaded her not to leave until God spoke directly to her about returning and confirmed the move with us back in Narok. Mary obsessively loved me and I was obsessed with her. She also adoringly loved our children and had never left them behind for such along time. But, just as in 1984 when she was left behind in Washington, she was again running out of patience with my insistence that she stay away from me. But because we firmly trusted each other and were sure of God's will to relocate us, she decided to wait upon Him a little longer.

MARY GETS IN THE WRONG TRAIN BUT ENDS UP AT GOD'S PREORDAINED DESTINATION

During the last three of her five months in the United States, Mary was housed by two young ladies from Kenya living in Washington, D.C. From here, she decided to visit our best family friend, Apostle Harry Das, in Newport News, Virginia, but she learned that he was coming on a mission in DC visiting a church in the western part of the city. Apostle Das founded the Chrisco churches in Kenya, beginning with prayer meetings christened "Morning glory" in Nairobi in 1978, which Mary attended regularly as a member and a partner. Mary brought me to meet him after she asked him to bless us during our engagement in September 1979 in Nairobi Kenya. He also spoke a prophetic blessed future for us as a couple. The next time we saw him was in December 1983 when we visited his home in Newport News Virginia. As diplomats based in DC, we were already enjoying the blessings he had pronounced over us back in 1979.

A dear friend of ours, Clement Kambo, from our early days as youth evangelists in Kenya (see picture of Kambo and us 1974 crusade picture section) was visiting us at our home in DC, and Mary felt strongly urged in the spirit to bring him to meet Apostle Das. Brother Clement had shared with us a strong calling to the ministry, but he did not know exactly where to start. Mary thought she could introduce him as a potential associate back in Nakuru where he was based. The divine meeting of the Rev. Das and then Evangelist Clement Kambo in Newport News, facilitated by Mary and me, gave birth in 1987 to one of the largest Chrisco churches in Nakuru under Bishop Clement and his faithful wife and co-pastor, Lucy Kambo. Apostle Harry Das reaped where he had planted seeds back in 1979. Bishop Clement Kambo and Pastor Lucy Kambo a huge boost to the Chrisco ministry in Kenya. Their ministry is one of the leading lights in the country.

For Mary, a meeting with such a special acquaintance, Apostle Das at this time (1992) would be refreshing. They could recall a friendship dating back to small beginnings in 1978 during the morning glory prayer meeting in Nairobi where they first met. For that to happen, Mary needed to ride the Metrorail headed west, but unfamiliar with the route, she took a train going east and ended up at RFK Memorial Stadium in Washington. As soon as she alighted and realized that she was lost, Mary looked around and noticed a huge tent with a banner reading "Calvary Pentecostal Tabernacle Evangelist Outreach." Little did she know that the tent would become her "Burning bush" as in the call of Moses (Exodus 3:2 NKJV). She decided to go in there and listen to the preaching instead of worrying about the original plan. This was one of her fasting days, and she had little energy left, so she settled on a bench near the rear exit of the tent.

That night brother Wallace Heflin, director of the Prophetic Prayer Ministry, based in Ashland, Virginia, was to preach, but he had not yet begun. Mary was one of the first few to arrive. Just before praise and worship started, Heflin walked all the way back to where Mary was sitting. He thought she looked weary and lonely. Looking straight into her eyes, he said, "Sister, my name is Brother Heflin. What is your name and what brings you here?" She replied, "My name is Mrs. Mary Nkoyo. I am a born-again Christian from Kenya. I saw this tent and I decided to come and hear the word of God." Then brother Heflin asked, "Where is the rest of your family?" She replied, "My husband and two children are back in Kenya. I have been here in the US. This is my fifth month praying and believing God to help me find a way they can join me here."

As the time to start approached and other people started flocking into the tent, brother Heflin moved quickly into the most intriguing phase of their conversation and said, "Mary, I watched you from the moment you walked into the tent, and the Lord spoke to me that you had a need that I can meet, and so this is what I want you to do for me: will you be able to come back to the meeting around this same time tomorrow?" She said yes. "This is what I want you to do for me. Bring the full names of your husband and each of your children. I will write an invitation letter for each of them and have them notarized with my ministry seal, and then you will mail them to them, and with that they can apply for visas at the US Embassy in Kenya to join you. Would you be able to do that for me, Sister Mary?" he asked. "Yes, Brother Heflin," Mary replied quickly and excitedly.

After that evening meeting, Mary headed straight for her temporary residence and called me with the exciting news. Then she took a paper and pen and obediently and prayerfully did exactly what she had been instructed to do. The following day, she was the first to arrive and immediately handed the paper to brother Heflin. He thanked her and told her to come the same time the following day because the tent would be moving out soon. On the third day, as soon as she got to the tent, brother Heflin handed Mary three separate invitation letters, one in my full name, one in Caroline's, and one in Armstrong's. Each of the letters had an original ministry seal stamped and notarized by the Rev. Wallace Heflin.

Mary's next task was to figure out the securest and quickest means of delivering the letters to me in Nairobi. This was the precious gold she had been waiting and praying for. Coincidentally, Mary was at an advanced stage working with a team of missionaries who were visiting Kenya, led by Margareta Williams, an old family friend from the time we served as diplomats (see our picture with Margareta and husband 1983) in Fredericksburg. She was based in Fredericksburg, Virginia. They were supposed to leave in June 1992, and Mary had asked me if I could convey them in our Mercedes-Benz to all the places they needed to speak and to interpret for them. After all, our children were in a boarding school and

I was free to do evangelism. By the time Mary needed a way of delivering the invitations to me, I had already made a commitment to take care of the missionaries during their three-week visit.

These events were all divine coincidences: my guests would be now the ones entrusted with hand delivery of the most important mail from America to me. Margareta not only conveyed the invitations by hand but also gave me a love gift of two thousand dollars cash on arrival ($2,000.00). With those invitations and the cash, I had processed passports, applied for and been issued three R-category visas by July 15, 1992—one for me and one for each of my children to travel to the United States, all stamped on individual passports. Talk of a promise-keeping God. With Mary already there and our travel visas in our pockets, we were all as good as being in America.

AFTER EIGHT YEARS OF USE THE MERCEDES BECOMES THE "JET" TO BRINGS US BACK TO USA

The next huddle was to raise money for three air tickets and other travel expenses for the three of us in the shortest time possible, a month at most. The camp meetings in Ashland, Virginia, through which we had been invited would be over by the end of September. But God had all things preordained and had made provision eight years prior. It came in the form of the Mercedes-Benz that I had I wanted to surrender to the DOD in 1984 but Mary had prevailed on me to keep. This was the same car that I had tried desperately to sell or to trade in for eight years from the moment it arrived from Germany in 1984, but Mary, through prayer and fasting, had blocked every potential buyer and trade-in deal.

Suddenly, the car bought us air tickets, covered all other travel expenses, and gave us pocket money. I had enough liquid cash to pay off all the debts that we had accumulated over time and to give my father a thirty-thousand-shilling gift. He was the only one among our family and close friends to whom I confided my plans to move to the United States. Mary and I agreed we sell her treasured jewel, and miraculously a buyer showed up in the same month. He was an immensely wealthy man from Nakuru, Kenya, who did not need to borrow from a bank to buy my expensive Benz. He had seen it for the first time during my visit to say good-bye to one of his relatives and our best family friends.

All these events took place in July 1992, soon after we secured our travel visas, and all we needed now were air tickets worth hundreds of thousands of shillings. From our friends home, where I was visiting, my host called his relative, telling him that I was looking for a buyer for my car to raise money to travel to America in a month's time. His relative then invited us to his mansion just a few minutes' drive from there. He came outside to meet us, and after walking around my car, he asked me how much money I wanted for it. I gave him a figure and the deal was sealed on the spot, based on my quote. He welcomed us to his house, and as soon as we sat down for a cup of tea, he took a briefcase I happened to be carrying with a few documents inside and went to his bedroom where he stashed hundreds of thousands of shillings in bundles of hundred-shilling bills in my brief case

Suddenly, it felt like a good dream and a bad dream at the same time: good in that I had suddenly acquired more than enough cash to travel and to settle all my debts, bad in that I would never again call this most cherished jewel our property again. I was happy and sad at the same time. In the twinkle of an eye, the Mercedes-Benz we had bought while in America eight years earlier, a car that Mary jealously guarded all those years from every attempt I made to dispose of it, became the "Jet" as it were that would bear us on its wings back to the United States. The briefcase that carried our miracle still sits on my desk twenty-two years later as I write, stuffed with all our family documents dating back to 1954 the year I was born.

The next most intriguing part of the deal came when the man who was ready to part with all that money to purchase the car asked me if I needed to use it to finalize my travel arrangements. I did not expect this question, but I answered yes. Scripture teaches that if you have favor with God, you will find favor with man: "And so find favor and high esteem in the sight of God and man" (Proverbs 3:4 NKJV). Showing favor and generosity I did not anticipate, the buyer told me to use the car until my last day in the country and not to consider the risks that offer entailed. He trusted me because of our years of friendship with his relative. Transfer of ownership never became an issue either. He simply said, "You may use the car until the last day, and once you are done, just drop it here with the key and a signed transfer, I will do the rest of the paperwork when I get to it." That is exactly what I did on August 10, 1992.

On August 14, 1992, my children and I walked through the US immigration gates in New York more than four months after Mary walked through the same gates on March 29, 1992. We found our hero Mary waiting and a Christian friend who offered to help her pick us up. They were waiting at the exit. It was an emotional reunion as we hugged and kissed. Four-and-a-half months had become an eternity because we had never been separated that long since our marriage in 1979.

I held my children's hands and prayed that God would bless them in this foreign land, a land of opportunity to which God had brought us, so someday they would become a blessing to children they left behind in Kenya. All the while, I was looking at the person who meant the world to me, Mary, my faithful, loving, and dedicated wife and the mother of my children. Here we were, standing on the same spot—all four of us— because she faithfully fasted and prayed and obediently followed God's lead to open these gates so we could enter and join her. We were all forever indebted to her, a debt we could never pay any other way but to love her every day.

After a two-week stopover in Massachusetts, we left for our next destination, the Calvary Pentecostal Tabernacle ministry campground in Ashland, Virginia. We were to remain there until the camp was over at the end of September. Great things happened while we attended the camp meetings, the main being the revival in which we found ourselves immersed. It was refreshing and the best place to start our journey of faith into the unknown. All these plans had been made by Mary, who covered every detail prior to our arrival. Mary never left anything to chance. She would pray for God's lead and then go after answers by faith. Mary had a very interesting spiritual characteristic, she knew when to pray and patiently wait for an answer and then she also knew when to pray and go for the instant answer without wait. Over my years with her, I watched this very unique phenomenon, sometimes I thought she was too aggressive while at others being too passive but in each case I proved myself wrong and she was right. That is why I often made this statement jokingly about her, "Even when Mary is wrong she is right."

A $350 KEY UNLOCKS GOD'S TREASURIES FOR 17 SOLID YEARS

A strong theme throughout the meetings at CPT Camp meeting 1992 was giving from our want and trusting God to supply all our needs according to His riches. And a voice of conviction started brewing strongly inside of me to give away all the little remaining cash that we had been allowed by the foreign exchange in Nairobi to bring over. We had been allowed only $250 per person, totaling $750. I had about $350 remaining in my pocket for the whole family when something divine but dangerous in the form of a voice of conviction, a still small voice, started saying, "That money in your pockets will not meet all the needs facing your family at the moment. But used as a seed, it will multiply and go a long way." In my spirit, the argument made a lot of sense because I had seen the truth of this many times before, but in my flesh, this was a suicidal thought I should not entertain, let alone dare tell Mary, who had no money left in her pockets, in spite of her great faith. God had to talk to her directly on this. Nor did I think I should let the children know I was contemplating giving away their portions of the balance in my pocket.

While I was still pondering this matter, Mary made an appointment with brother Heflin so she could bring us to meet him (see pictures of the day at CPT in the picture section). We felt joy at meeting the man whom God had used in a miraculous way to reunite us in America. I thought of Mary's obedience to God's voice during the time she was in the United States alone, meeting individuals like brother Heflin who would become instrumental in our resettlement in the land God had promised us years back. In this camp alone, where she had retreated for two weeks of fasting and prayer prior to our arrival, she had made many contacts. As soon as brother Heflin saw the four of us through his office window, he rushed to welcome us. He told us that he had been to Kenya on a missionary tour and liked the country.

This was a short discussion because so many people had to see brother Heflin on this campus hosting more than five hundred people at a time, many wanting to visit with him daily for a word of prophecy. He held my hands in his huge hands and suddenly delivered a prophetic word of knowledge about great doors that God was about to open for my family.

Toward the end, he spoke as if ordering me, saying, "Do not leave this country until God says you can—until His full purpose for bringing you and your family to the US is accomplished." I was shocked to hear the rumbling and authoritative voice of the man whose signature on a letter with the seal of his ministry became instrumental in our coming to America. But over and above that, he had accommodated my family among the hundreds of others with our own rooms and with food, telling me, "You are welcome to stay until God says it is time to move and where to move." In a nutshell, Brother Heflin not only invited us to the United States, but we were welcome to stay at CPT beyond the Camp meeting on full board until God had opened doors for our next move.

That evening a guest speaker again emphasized the theme of giving to God from our needs in exchange for the key to His treasure. Mary and I were sitting with the kids on the tabernacle benches, listening to the preacher. (Normally one of us would be at the front on the floor worshipping and praising, while the other would be sitting on the benches with the kids.) At the end of his sermon, based on the story of the widow of Zarephath (1 Kings 17:7–16), he asked how many wanted to challenge God with their "not enough" for His "more than enough." How many wanted to test God as the widow of Zarephath had done by giving to Elijah all the food she had by making an offering for the work of ministry to others in need and trusting God to meet their own needs more sufficiently like the widow in the story?

Those words pricked me like spikes in my soul as I again contemplated offering the $350 for the needs of others so that God could meet ours. The Spirit of God made it clear to me that this was the moment to tell Mary because the atmosphere and the timing were right. All of us, including the children, had heard the message, so I did not have to convince them. As people started filing past the preacher with their offerings, I told my family that this was our moment to test God and that although all we had was what I was holding in my trembling hands, we should be ready and in agreement to part with it. As soon as I said that, my heart ceased to see dollar value in the $350 and what it could buy. Instead, I saw the invaluable opportunities that God would bring to us if we moved in obedience.

By nature, when overwhelmed, Mary would offer little in the way of opinion. All she said was that if I was sure that God had clearly spoken

88

to me on the matter, then I should obey. That was what I was waiting to hear. Had she opposed making the offering, I would not have done it. With everyone on board, there was power in agreement. I dashed to the front, dropped all my money into the preacher's open hands, and walked back to my family, feeling great relief that I had finally obeyed the prompting of the Holy Spirit.

A few days after this encounter, we found ourselves sitting opposite a beautiful black couple at breakfast. They had driven all the way from Alexandria, Virginia, to attend a power-packed weekend revival rally. Some of the most powerful evangelists in the country would be invited for weekend rallies at the camp. As a result, nonresident campers would flood the campgrounds. The couple told us they had been coming two to three weekends a month, depending on the guests. Their names were Vernon and Janice Dunlap. The wife reminded me of Rev. Terecia Wairimu of TWEM back in Kenya, while the husband reminded me of Lamont, the "Son" on the popular *Sanford and Son* comedy show. In the course of our fellowship over breakfast, the Dunlaps became curious about our plans. We told them of our desire to attend a Bible college so we could be equipped for our calling to ministry. They asked if we had found an opening at a college, and we said that since we had just recently arrived, we had not made any progress in that respect.

We would soon discover that meeting the Dunlaps was a God-ordained appointment. They told us of the church they attended in Fort Washington, Maryland, just across the Potomac River from where they lived in Alexandria. The church, under the Church of God denomination based in Knoxville, Tennessee, was sponsoring a Bible institute that was offering full scholarships to many foreign students and local residents on Theological courses. They said that they were already enrolled and that they knew the college president, Dr. T. L. Lowery, also the senior pastor of the church, and the dean, Dr. Snowden, and could introduce us to them so that we could be given full scholarships to attend.

The next question was how we would get there. We had no transportation. The Dunlaps proposed that the following weekend we take the campus van, which ran between Ashland and Washington, to their residence in Alexandria and stay with them over the weekend. That would enable us to go to church with them on Sunday so we could tour the campus. On Monday morning, they would take us to meet the dean for an interview and possible admission.

That Monday morning, we left the dean's office with full two-year scholarships. All we needed to do was to turn in all our documents for a change of status from visitor to student visas and to student dependents for our children. The only hurdle remaining was where to stay because accommodations for married students were no longer available. We had two adolescent children, complicating the issue. If we were simply a couple, we might have split up in singles rooms until family accommodations became available. But God knew our need, and soon He would come through for us in an amazing and most powerful way because we had looked to the needs of others.

So we had secured full scholarships and a promise to change our immigration status from religious visitor to student under the religious vocational category, but we needed accommodations outside the campus to show to Immigration a legitimate residential address for the processing. With all that, that took place on our first trip outside the campgrounds, we started seeing the doors of opportunity begin to open in line with the word of knowledge from brother Heflin. We had no money left, but our dear and longtime friend Margarita Williams from Fredericksburg, Virginia, visited us at the Camp ground and without asking, she would provide us with pocket money from time to time. She would also pick us up and bring us to her home about forty-five minutes from Ashland.

THE FIRST HOME OF A WEALTHY WIDOW OPENS IN SPRINGFIELD, VIRGINIA

Just a few days before the end of that summer camp meeting at Calvary Pentecostal Tabernacle, we started trying to figure out where to move next. We were still under the limited religious visitor visas because despite having been offered full scholarships, we needed a residential address to process the change of status to student visa. The college would not indicate a nonexistent residential address in its application for us, but God had a plan for our lives. He knew where we were going to stay, how long we would stay there, what we would eat and drink, and its proximity to our college and to schools for our two beautiful children, who by law had to be enrolled by October 1992.

One evening, Mary asked me to come with her to a public telephone booth outside the camp's main office. She reached into her purse and took out her treasured notebook with telephone contacts for the families and friends she had met during her five-month tour. She turned to one of the pages and told me about an elderly widow who had hosted her a few months earlier. They met during a three-day ladies convention Mary had attended in Washington. At the end of the day, resident attendees would host guests in their homes if the guests did not have hotel rooms. Mary was hosted by a seventy-two-year-old widow named Mary Ford. She lived by herself in a huge five-bedroom home in Springfield, Virginia.

My wife said the lady was friendly and had asked to meet our family when we arrived in America. What Mary Ford did not know was that while Mary was visiting, she would spend most of the night praying and asking God that when her family arrived, we would be hosted there until we could find our own place. After all, this elderly lady was not using most of her home. Mary had a confirmation in her spirit that this was the place God wanted us to be until we were more independent and that evening, by prompting of the Holy Spirit, she remembered that encounter and prayer at Mary Ford's home.

Mary dialed the phone number, and she and Mary Ford began a friend-to- friend conversation, first trying to remember where they had met. At last, Mary got to the most important point. "My family is finally here, Mary, and we are at Calvary Pentecostal Tabernacle. I would like to bring them to greet you. Would you be available, say, tomorrow afternoon? Mary asked. "I just came from the hospital today where I was admitted for the last two weeks, but you can come and visit for three days," answered Mary Ford faintly. That alone was a huge miraculous step, and when we returned to our room, we held hands and thanked God for giving us the place He had prepared for our stay until we could find our own. The widow of Zarephath opened her home to sustain the prophet Elijah during the lean years in Israel (1 Kings 17:7–16 NIV). Accordingly, the first widow of Springfield will open her home for the Nkoyo family in their lean years in America.

We packed our belongings and asked the camp to give us a one-way van ride to Springfield, Virginia over that weekend. The van driver wanted to know whether we had been there before and if we could easily identify the residence. Mary gave him the address and said that when we got to the neighborhood she would know the house. We arrived around 2 p.m. the following day and found Mary Ford waiting for us, but the moment we removed our belongings from the van and the van left, she got a little worried. She saw all these belongings as a clear sign that we intended to stay for quite a while, and she said something like, "Did y'all move?" We avoided answering directly as Mary, the family spokesperson started introducing us.

As soon as we moved our belongings into the house, Mary Ford shared the sad story of how she had fallen sick and been hospitalized. She was still recovering, and we prayed a special prayer for her to get well quickly. She said that prayer would be a source of comfort during our stay, not mentioning how long she thought that stay would be. But as time passed, God showered her heart with love and passion for us as we ministered to her physical and spiritual needs daily and told her we had come to America to get equipped for the work of ministry. We told her about the scholarship we had been offered but the limitations due to accommodations.

She asked if we could stay six more days so we could have deeper fellowship, and during that time she opened her heart to us, telling the details of what had led to her sudden sickness. I believe God brought us to that home not just to provide for us, but to heal Mary, giving her a loving family that she would later always fondly call "my family from Kenya." She also needed daily spiritual nourishment through fellowship in the Scripture. Our needs and her needs coincided. The three-day visit turned to 730 days, two solid years. From October 1992 to December 1994, we became an essential part of Mary Ford's family, and her church, the Assembly of God church in Springfield under Pastor Wendell Cover, became our church and he became our pastor. The church would often give her love gifts to support our stay with her which Mary ford never even needed.

Now in a matter of about two weeks, from the day I placed $350 in the hands of the preacher, we had full scholarship offers, a change of status and a prophet Elijah package deal in the home of Mary Ford. Her home became the residential address that the college used to apply to change our religious visitor status to student status and also the address for our children admission to American system of schools. Our new home was a fifteen-minute drive from the Bible institute in Fort Washington, Maryland; a five-minute walk from Caroline's school, Washington Irving Middle School, and a five-minute School Bus ride from Armstrong's Rolling Valley Elementary School. The bus picked him up every morning from outside our new home. Soon after, we had our own car to go to College and get around places with Mama Ford our host because she could not drive.

This is a brief description of Mary Ford's home from a Realtor's perspective: "A home nestled in a quiet neighborhood; conveniently located near schools, shopping and restaurants; Lake Accotink, Burke Lake, Hidden Pond and other parks are minutes away. 5 beds, 2.5 baths, 2,600 sq. ft."

I felt like a married son with a family living in the home of his well-to-do widowed mother. She became Mama Ford to me and Mary, and grandma to Armstrong and Caroline. Wherever we went, including our home church of close to two thousand members, she would proudly introduce us as "my family from Kenya," and although she was white, she became to us a reincarnation of my hero mother, who had passed a year earlier. She treated us as my mother would, and we quickly adapted to her. In their schools, our children told their peers and their teachers that they lived with their grandmother. But the name sounded American yet they still had fresh African accents, especially Armstrong, who was struggling with the English language. Whenever teachers called the home, the person answering the phone was an American senior citizen. Mary Ford also visited the children in school, and the administration came to recognize her as their grandmother.

Mary Ford made it a point to tell her sons and her daughter, who lived with their families elsewhere in the country, that she had found company in a family from Kenya and that we had become part of her life. That could have implied a threat to their inheritance, but they were happy to know that we had come into their elderly mother's live at a critical moment, soon after her physical attack. They got to meet us when they came to visit, and we had a lively exchange as if we were one big family.

In the large home, a self-contained room was assigned to me and Mary. Caroline and Armstrong each had a room. A spacious carpeted basement was our main family hangout, a place where the children could play, and the living room and dining room upstairs were open to all of us. We had access to every part of the home including Mama Ford's bedroom. We were just like any cohesive, happy family. As soon as my status changed and was authorized to work we bought a car, Mama Ford, who did not drive, was assured of getting around because I could take her to places.

We never got to see a bill of any kind or to learn the cost of groceries, because Mama Ford would not let us see what it cost her to feed four extra mouths. Every two weeks I would take her to the Giant grocery store in the neighborhood, and she would spend two to three hours picking out quality groceries for her new enlarged family. My job was to push two to three large shopping carts fully loaded with all kinds of high-quality and healthy food and cleaning materials into my car and to unload them when we got home. She would not let me see the check she wrote at the checkout, which I knew was in excess of two hundred dollars at a time.

Even more humbling, every Friday, she would do all our laundry when we were in school and at college, fold it, and place it on top of our beds. But most of all, when my wife fell sick, suffering from depression, Mary Ford turned into the mother of a sick daughter and did everything she could, working with us to get Mary the best medical help possible. She did this after making a thorough enquiry about involuntary hospitalization for a patient of depression. Working together as family, we requested help and went through the judicial process. Mary Ford gave evidence on the fears we had that my wife's failure to eat for lengthy periods was endangering her life.

Just like any mother, Mary Ford gave me and my children motherly and grandmotherly emotional support throughout that time of great uncertainty. She offered our family warmth and comfort. We did not have to worry about what to eat or to drink or about a roof over our heads. Mary Ford did not regard my part-time job earnings as anything other than pocket change to take my children and my wife out on a weekend and to fuel my vehicle to and from college. I can say with confidence that while we had the prophet Elijah's provision package, our budget was four times his and covered much more. When the preacher at Calvary Pentecostal

Tabernacle challenged us to surrender to others in need what was "not enough" to us, we dared believe that God would supply all our needs to the point where we would have more than enough. That is exactly what He did for 730 days in a row. We proved the truth of the promise in Scripture: "And my God shall supply all your need according to His riches in glory by Christ Jesus" (Philippians 4:19 NKJV).

When it became obvious that we had to move to our own apartment in Alexandria, a neighboring city, Mary Ford was devastated. She had become attached to her adopted Kenyan family, but it was absolutely necessary for us to move so that my wife could have freedom to run her own home like every independent woman. She had been used to doing this since we were married sixteen years earlier. However, this was not the last we would hear from the generous widow. In 1996, while in Alexandria, Mary felt a desire to return to Kenya on a ministry outreach. She had been ordained as a minister of the gospel earlier the same year. We organized a fundraiser for her trip and invited our friends. One of those who turned up was Mary Ford. She gave Mary a thousand dollars toward her air ticket. The trip never took place, because Mary went down for a second time with a devastating depression attack.

In retrospect I see Mary Ford's gesture as a parting gift from the first widow to the Nkoyo family and as a link between the first and the second wealthy widow, whom God would use to plant seeds that would have a permanent effect. The original seed, $350, given away to meet the needs of others in an act of faith and obedience became more than enough. It would continue to unlock the treasuries of wealthy widows and have a lasting impact on future generations of the Nkoyo family.

THE PURSE OF A WEALTHY WIDOW OPENS IN ALEXANDRIA, VIRGINIA

Throughout 1995, we lived in the Friendship Apartments complex off of Richmond Highway in Alexandria, and in the beginning of 1996 we bought our first home, a brand-new trailer home sixty feet by thirty feet with two bedrooms and two bathrooms, and moved to Audubon Estate in Alexandria. These moves boosted Mary's pride and joy greatly and relieved her depression. She began a new life in Alexandria and a powerful work of ministry, especially after her ordination in the same year by Dr. John Kivuva.

Under the auspices of our Christian Heritage Ministries International, Mary organized power-packed evangelistic meetings in hotels and spoke or invited speakers. She became well known in the area, but her struggles with depression often slowed her down. Whenever she became overconfident and lax about taking her antidepressants, she would go down and take a painfully slow time to fully recover. That happened in the second half of 1996, and it was about two years before she was up and running strong again.

In Alexandria, God continued His miraculous providence to us through wealthy widows. He brought us Jo Gummelt a resident of Alexandria. She was sixty-four when we met in 1996 in a kind of divine takeover from where Mary Ford had left off. This is the widow whom God would use to bring us real wealth (property ownership), intellectual wealth (further education for our children), and American citizenship. Above all, she offered a motherly/grandmotherly love the way Mary Ford had. Mrs. Gummelt remained a part of our lives for the rest of her life on earth. Long after we left Virginia and moved to Texas, we stayed in constant contact, and she would often send her love gifts to us.

In her last week before passing on to glory in October 2009, I made a trip from Texas to Alexandria to see her at the nursing home where she was in a coma. For health reasons Mary was not able to join me. Just like Mary whenever I walked into her ICU at Baylor Medical Center in June 2014 or my mother, who was in a coma during her last two months at Narok Hospital in 1991, Mrs. Gummelt radiated joy and moved her head as I entered her room, calling out "Mama Jo" as I always did. All she could do was move her head and her lips in response as if calling my name Wilfred, as she always fondly did. Her only son, who was in twenty-four-hour attendance, was amazed at these gestures. I massaged her neck, her back, and her arms, hugged her, prayed, and anointed her with oil. My visit lasted two days, a Wednesday and a Thursday, and I spent hours by her bedside each time. On Friday, October 23, when I arrived back in Waco, Texas, we received news that she had passed on to glory that same day.

This was the last wealthy widow phenomenon in Nkoyo family that lasted seventeen years from the time it was prophesied by a man named Paul Adams in Massachusetts. His family hosted us for the first two weeks after our arrival from Kenya in August 1992. This was our first stop before moving to the Ashland campgrounds in Virginia in September of that year. Mary had met Paul and his family previously at the campgrounds and requested if they could host us. On our last day with the family as we were praying, Brother Paul Adams spoke under the anointing of the Holy Spirit saying that God was going to open a door into the home of a wealthy widow through whom He would meet all our needs.

Little did we know how many widows we would encounter or how long a period this would be. These ladies were unmistakable manifestations of God's providence, mothers to us and grandmothers to our children, who always fondly referred to them as their grandmas even though the two ladies were of white race and quite different from our African race, color did not stand in our way of relationship between us. Remarkably, whenever Mary went down with depression, each of these ladies treated her as their own daughter. Jo Gummelt would come to our home, get Mary into her expensive Lincoln limousine, and take her for a mother-daughter day out. During such outings, she would persuade Mary to resume her antidepressants.

This phenomenon was also a fulfillment of words given to me on September 25, 1988. They came at a time when we were at a kind of T-junction and unsure whether to turn right or left. This was soon after I made a leap of faith by ending my twelve years of military service with only a vague plan B. On that early misty morning in a rented home (the former Red Hill Motel in Limuru, Kenya), I was sitting at our family breakfast table by myself when I randomly turned to a page in the Bible and read this passage: "Kings shall be your foster fathers, and their queens your nursing mothers; they shall bow down to you with their faces to the earth, and lick up the dust of your feet. Then you will know that I am the Lord, for they shall not be ashamed who wait for Me" (Isaiah 49:22–23 NKJV). The still small voice impressed upon me to take note, highlight that passage, and share it with Mary.

FROM VISITOR TO US CITIZENSHIP

Scripture says that "we know that all things work together for good to them that love God, to them that are the called according to His purpose" (Romans 8:28 NKJV). To the Nkoyos, "all things" must mean the sweet and the bitter coming together to change our destiny as a family. My experience twelve years earlier during my service in Washington was a painful one. I was recalled abruptly and was put through painful questioning on allegations of treason fabricated by individuals envious of my progress. Initially, my appointment as assistant military attaché was the sweetest gift the DOD could have given me. This was and still is something accessible to only a select few. The appointment come with many benefits that suddenly changed the status of the appointee. That was why the few fortunate ones like me became targets of envy and were subjected to witch hunts.

However, my nightmare in 1984 was short-lived by God's grace and protection, and the apparently quick end of the story brought great material gain. However, unknown to all of us, that was not the end, but only the beginning. God had a grander future gain in store. It would come in 2007, twenty-three years later. The stigma inflicted upon me by the treason charges would lead to approval for asylum in the United States for me and my family in May 1995, a change to permanent residence in 2000, and to naturalized citizenship in 2007. Scripture puts it in a better perspective: "For I know the thoughts that I think toward you, saith the Lord, thoughts of peace, and not of evil, to give you an expected end" (Jeremiah 29:11 KJV).

I revisit this experience because whereas the issue had appeared and disappeared quickly for lack of evidence, the stigma remained for as long as I was in military uniform. I applied for early retirement (1988 at 34 years of age) and became a private citizen, but that move reactivated history, substance or no substance, and I became a person of interest to the political system. The government of the day was an insecure institution, particularly allergic to anything American and anyone inclined toward America. From the moment I ceased to report to an immediate superior authority, I became a person to be watched closely whether in Limuru, where I had relocated and prospered, or in my hometown where I tried to reestablish myself after the incident in Limuru. Wherever I was and whatever I was doing, private eyes watched my every move. In the early '90s, my parents confided in me their fears for my safety and that of my family.

The political philosophy of the day was, "Either you are with us or against us." Quiet behavior and lack of involvement were considered hostility in disguise. The Kenyan Police Special Branch and Central Intelligence Department would question my parents to try to find out what I was up to and who my associates were. However, they would get the same answer every time: "Our son's closest confidante is his wife, and his associates are fellow Christians, found where he goes to church. That is the only place you will find him because he does not visit social places like bars or nightclubs." The more my parents kept reporting these encounters to me, the more fearful I became of a system that could fabricate anything about people and had the power to arrest or abduct them. I had known of a few cases, but one in particular concerned a family friend, Mr. K from Nakuru. He was arrested under circumstances similar to mine and died as a torture victim in a police cell shortly after his arrest.

I pondered these things. I was fearful but tried to keep my wife from unnecessary worries, recalling her ordeal in Washington in 1984. But deep in my heart I knew that a safe future was not guaranteed in Kenya for me and my family. I welcomed any opportunity to leave with my wife and children. When I landed in New York on August 14, 1992, my fears evaporated. I prayed for my children and said in my heart, *I am here to stay.* A new life began for me (notably in August, month eight, the number of new beginnings).

That nightmarish moment in May 1984 at the office of the top Kenya's general, when I had to respond to treasonous allegations while in Washington, turned into immediate material gain. And, four years after my retirement in 1992, God would use the enduring stigma of those charges to make my case for asylum to the US Immigration and Naturalization Service. In the end, my family became inheritors of the same nation my persecutors wanted to remove me from. Today, none of them is left in the United States, and the majority are dead and forgotten as I confirmed through obituaries.

Our long journey to citizenship began as soon as we established a residential base in the home of Mary Ford early in 1993. From here I launched my application and by January 2000 we were granted green-card status. Jo Gummelt, who had become the embodiment of the widow of Zarephath since our arrival in Alexandria, gave us a Christmas surprise in 2006. She decided to sponsor our whole family, five of us, for citizenship, offering to pay all the filing fees. She had sponsored Caroline for Baylor University in 1999 soon after we met at a Bible study hosted in her home.

Jo Gummelt loved us as a family. She made a motherly long-distance call to Texas where we had moved, asking whether we had filed for citizenship, and when I said no, she wanted to know what was holding us back. I told her that I had other more pressing financial needs and since we already had our green cards, investment into citizenship application would be my next project. She asked me if I was ready to fill out an application for each of my family members, including Caroline and her husband, Daniel Waithaka, living in Atlanta, Georgia. The moment I said I coul, she said, "You do the paperwork and let me do the check." That is how we transitioned from visitor visa holders to naturalized citizens, becoming co-heirs with the born citizens of the most prosperous nation on earth.

Going even further back to 2004, Jo Gummelt loaned me $20,000 for down- payment and repair expenses in a fixer-upper real estate investment here in Waco Texas. A friend and I bought three properties in a package deal. Each of us needed to raise $8,500. When my adopted mama learned about this, she loaned me more than double the amount to enable me to fix the properties. In the end the properties were worth more than $250,000. For our mansion in Waco, she loaned me $15,000 toward renovation costs. It is worth more than $200,000.

I am not ashamed to acknowledge America as a land of uniquely benevolent people and opportunities but also one that God promised to bring my family to inherit. He spoke to my wife and me about this land in August 1988 in Limuru where we had moved after I retired from the army. He described the land through Deuteronomy 8:7–14, and in August 1992, exactly four years later, we were all standing firmly on that Promised Land with our arrival in New York City. God is faithful. He used a three-month window of opportunity in Mary's forgotten visitor visa, sending my faithful wife, a prayer warrior and an obedient follower of God's lead, to open the door so our family and posterity could attain to the promise He made to us in Limuru.

MARY, A RELENTLESS CHASER OF GOD'S PROMISE FOR HER FAMILY

God honored Mary's spiritual endurance. She was tested while alone for more than four months in the United States chasing after His promise and was found not wanting. She was true to her husband, her children, and her friends. Mary loved me with every cell in her body, and I loved her the same way. We kept our promise to each other because we were indebted to God for each other, indebted to each other, to our children, and to our friends. God used Mary's faith, faithfulness, and commitment to her marriage and to her family to open a narrow gap through which we marched into the land He promised us.

When Mary passed on to glory in June 2014, I had no second thoughts about a more preferred country or place to lay her remains to rest. It would be the land of promise and a central place within driving distance of each of the family members she loved and who loved her in return. America was that country and the place was Blue Bonnet Hills Memorial Park in Colleyville, Texas. And that is where I also made my wish public (see pictures in the picture section), choosing a spot next to my high school sweetheart. When that time comes and I move on to join her in glory, my remains will be laid next to hers as a symbol of our reunion on earth and in eternity, where we shall never be separated by time or space even for a second. I and generations of my family are forever indebted to Mary for pioneering the way to the land of promise, a preordained inheritance for us.

PART 4

Mary's Faith at work in a Complex Final Move

CHAPTER 7

Opening New Doors of Opportunity (2011 to Present)

Mary's hallmark was a childlike faith. After praying at night on issues of great concern to both of us, she would quickly sleep like a baby. Just like children certain that their parents will keep vigil over them while they sleep, Mary was sure that the God who never slumbers would not only keep watch over her but would supply all that she asked for in her prayers.

My story was quite different. Instead of sleeping, I lay awake in bed or paced the floor as I wrestled with possible solutions to the issue over which we just prayed. More often than not, the soldier in me would get louder than the saint, saying, "A soldier must pray always, with his eyes open to keep track of the enemy; his boots on and his gun slung over his shoulder at ready for action anytime. A soldier prays on the move to the place of action. He cannot sit, standstill, or slumber on the frontline." I would further justify this attitude by quoting the scripture, "Keep awake, and pray that you may not enter into temptation...." (Matthew 26:41 WNT). To a Christian, this world with all the evils going on today, it is a typical frontline.

Mary's sleep would be disrupted by my movements, and she would wake up wondering why I was pacing the floor or writing down plans. I would often ask her to pray for me and even beg her to lay hands on me to calm my nerves. She would sometimes grant my request, but more often than not she would say I didn't need more prayers, because God had already heard us the first time we prayed, and all we needed to do was to wait to receive His answer. But for the soldier in me, that was too simplistic. She would persuade me to calm down and sleep, assuring me that God would respond to us in His time. She was always right because no matter how long it took, we would receive His answer.

Mary always challenged my preconceived notions, which were based on my cultural and military value system and upbringing. She would always remind me that God does not need our help to bring to pass what He has promised or what we seek in our prayers. But while I agreed with her, my biggest weakness was my impatience. I have a problem with patience because of the speed at which I like getting things done. Mary was never in a hurry but always remained deliberate unless the Holy Spirit prompted urgency in her. In that case, she would move quickly and with boldness for answers here and now. She would fast until God told her exactly what to do and where to position herself to receive the desired request.

I developed great respect and admiration for all these characteristics in Mary yet I could never become Mary but thank God she was mine. She may have appeared tardy in getting to the end of a matter, but slowly but surely she would get there. Over the years, I came to see Mary as my trusted pastor, prophet, and priest. She was a source of great inspiration and assurance to me. She calmed many storms in my life by humbly rebuking me, saying, "Slow down my love, the world will not come to an end!" or "If it does not work out today, it will work out tomorrow." When Mary was down with depression and withdrawn, I spent long stretches in a spiritual wilderness without prophetic words, pastoral counseling, or priestly services in my life. To illustrate Mary's boldness and practical faith, her patience and confidence in God, I will share an episode from her last mile on earth the outcome of which will affect future generations of our family and friends.

MARY LEADS THE WAY TO THE DALLAS-FORT WORTH AREA

In August 2012, Mary took a bold step of faith while in Atlanta, Georgia, where she was visiting with our daughter Caroline's family. She knew she could not return to Waco, Texas, because all the area's kidney clinics and doctors had decided not to continue her treatment, mainly because of her lack of cooperation. (Depression always worked against her consistency in staying on kidney treatment.) She asked me if we could relocate to the Dallas-Irving area. That was a tall order for several reasons. First, we would have to leave behind our mansion in which we had invested most of our life's savings and a great deal of labor. I was not willing to rent it out even though we still carried a mortgage on it. I feared damage by tenants, which is common. Second, I would have to resign from my job in Waco and hunt for work in the Dallas-Fort Worth area. Third, I would need to look for a clinic acceptable to Mary for her dialysis treatment and hope she would remain compliant. Fourth, we would have to find an apartment in a secure area and one that met her standards.

Mary was always a woman of class but at the same time thrifty throughout our life together. She had ways of shopping for less and making the most out of it. Mary was so beautiful that even dressed in old-fashioned clothes, she still appeared elegant. Her home would look as if it were expensively decorated because of the way she used bargain items picked up at yard sales and Goodwill store outlets. Mary could have worn rags and found in a village market place and I would still be attracted to her beauty, decency, and Godly-fear. Scripture show us that it was not special apparel, cosmetics, or jewelry that made the king prefer Esther the "slave" girl above all women but the basics (Esther 2:12–17 NKJV). That was my high school sweetheart—basically, naturally beautiful and low maintenance! This is a fact many who knew her in her early days, especially after conversion would attest to.

For relocation to happen, the last three items had to converge at one convenient place and time: the clinic, the apartment, and a new job for me.

Over the years, I had learned to listen to Mary's words with the heart and the spirit and not to argue over issues on which we could not immediately agree. That included tough requests such as her proposal to move to the Dallas-Irving area. I let her continue before I responded. "Remember the time I stayed at the DFW Hotel in Irving, supporting the Benny Hinn Ministry in Grapevine, Texas?" she asked. "There is an excellent clinic on XY Street where I used to go for dialysis. I sincerely came to like both the staff and the standards of treatment there. Also, in that neighborhood there are good apartments. I would like you to check them out. Jobs in mid-cities areas are always plenteous, and you should be able to get a good job there within a short time. Please make arrangements for our relocation to Irving within the next thirty days when my visitor-privilege treatment here in Atlanta clinic ends."

My love and empathy for Mary had grown with time, especially as she struggled with complicated health issues. It would have been insensitive to hassle with her or to ignore her request before trying. And because I desired that Mary would live out her full life without stress from me, I had to remain open to such requests even if they sounded unworkable and complicated in terms of time frame and combinations like the one at hand. But as I promised to try, she committed to back me up with prayers. We always had a team style in getting things done even the most complex. In this particular puzzle according to me, hers was the hard part, to pray and mine was the easy part, to work.

I decided to start with a hunt for a clinic and not to search by phone but through random visits without necessarily making appointments. As I walked into the very first one she suggested in Irving, I met one of the nurses, who was rushing out on her way home after clocking out. Because no one was at the reception desk, I asked her if I could speak to the chief nurse. She asked me what I needed and if she could help, and I explained that I was checking to see if the clinic had a vacant seat based on the schedule Mary required. She told me that there was a vacant spot because a patient who had been on the same schedule had just relocated and that all Mary needed to do was to sign up for the seat before it was taken. Normally people have to be on a waiting list for a long time. I called Mary immediately and broke the news. She was excited and said she wished she could fly in the next day.

However, I still had to look for an apartment close by that would meet her standards for modesty and shopping convenience. Three miles down the street from the clinic, I discovered a beautiful ground-floor apartment that had just fallen vacant at the Knoll Woods complex also in Irving. I immediately submitted an application. I called Mary to notify her, giving her full description so that she would endorse my application. She did and was once again pleased.

Now I was down to the last piece of the puzzle, getting a convenient job with a flexible work schedule that would allow me to take Mary back and forth to treatment three times a week and other special health related appointments. Finding such a job became a test of our faith and patience, but I knew I could surely count on Mary's superior patience and her unshakable faith. I could not resign from my job in Waco before landing a new job in the Dallas-Fort Worth area. At the same time, we needed to wait for our apartment to be prepared for occupation after the former tenant left. That meant to secure the vacant seat at the clinic, we had to shuttle between Waco and Irving three times a week, a one-and-a-half-hour drive each way without traffic. In other words, each day she had treatment, a minimum of eight hours would go to travel and treatment alone! I had no time for a new job hunt. God had to do something out of the ordinary.

We continued to pray, believing God to intervene on the job situation, and in September 2012, something dramatic happened that would change not only our immediate circumstances, but continue to have an effect to this day as I do authors edit on this manuscript and long after. This event took place as a result of Mary's sensitivity and obedience to the leading of God.

One day during the third week of our fatiguing shuttles between Waco and Irving, we were driving to the clinic and were running late for the appointment. We came to a red light and stopped. From this point we could see a convenience store across the street, and Mary suddenly asked me to stop there and pick up a special advertisement magazine called *Green Sheet*. She said, "You can find the job you need in this publication." That was Mary's normal wordings on attainment of things she had committed to faith.

I resisted, arguing that we were late and risked her termination from treatment for noncompliance and that we could not afford to stop even for a minute to pick up any magazine. I said there were many other stores in the area and I could pick up the publication after dropping her off. But Mary became persistent, saying, "Don't worry about me getting to the clinic on time. After all, I am already late. These magazines go out from the shelves fast. You may not find any by the time you get to those other stores." Not desirous to irritate her, I gave up, pulled into the parking lot, picked up the magazine, tossed it onto the back seat, and sped off toward the clinic. My patience was on edge as I thought about how Mary's noncompliance in Waco had led us to where we were and how we were taking the same risks again.

As soon as I had left my wife at the clinic, after making a few apologies to the nurses for coming late, I headed to a library in Hurst, Texas. I needed to go online to research a college paper due that day. That had become my routine and the most convenient way to pass time as I waited during Mary's treatment. It would last four hours and then we would head back to Waco with another two hours on the road. But just before I could begin my research, my cell phone rang. It was Mary calling to find out whether I had checked through the magazine and what I had found. Since I could not lie to her, I said I hadn't checked, but I promised I would shortly. I got back to my research, but about two hours later, the phone rang again. It was Mary, asking me the same question.

This time, I decided to stop everything I was doing and quickly peruse the publication. However, nothing appeared to match my interests or skills. My patience was being tested to the max, but I searched again. This time, instead of rushing, I looked slowly, ad by ad, and lo and behold, on the bottom of the last page, I found a strong job possibility. Because Mary was still on the phone and would not let me go, I explained it to her. She said that such jobs were quite competitive and that I should call while the opening lasted. Reluctantly, I promised I would, and she said, "Let me end this call and you give them a call. Please let me know the outcome. Meanwhile, I will be praying for you."

I thought, *I better do it because my wife won't let me off the hook.* As soon as she let me go, I called the number and the opportunity was still open. For Mary's, sake, I headed straight there before the offices closed to interview. I made sure to call Mary on the way, asking for her prayers. But she responded, "Go and take the job because I have witness in my spirit that it is yours." This reminded me of Scripture: "Rise ye up, take your journey, and pass over the river Arnon: behold, I have given into thine hand … begin to possess it" (Deuteronomy 2:24 KJV).

As a result of Mary's patience, persistence, and bold faith, I got the job. My hourly pay started at more than one-and-a-half times what my Waco job offered and it came with all benefits. But most important, besides my employer life insurance coverage, Mary, as my dependent was given an automatic life insurance coverage, and though it was for a smaller amount, none of her complex health issues were put into consideration. That was rarity among life insurance companies. In addition, my work schedule was so flexible that I could go to college and take care of Mary's visits to clinics and all other doctor's appointments without a loss of work hours or benefits. Income from this job covered all the expenses at our apartment and our home mortgage in Waco and allowed us to make extra contributions toward ministries. My job with the company near DFW International Air Port was less than ten minute-drive from home and about five minutes from the clinic. But the greatest thing above all else concerning this company with hundreds of thousands of workers across the globe, is the working environment it has created for its workers. I may be wrong to assume that all the establishments are the same, but the environment at our establishment to me is the best in every aspect, that I have worked in since my years in Kenya armed forces. I always look forward to go to work, not just for the money but to be around all these wonderful people coming from almost every corner of the globe whose friendship and friendly smiles break the barriers of culture and language. The company which cater for hundreds of airlines across the globe has created unique opportunities for work to all willing and able men and women regardless of their age (legal), culture, nationality, religion, language or level of education. They all work as a happy team from top management down to the cleaners with so much respect and courtesy. I was privileged to be part of that team. And when my wife passed these kind workmates, who have become like my own brothers and sisters, reached out to me with words of comfort and financial assistance towards my wife's funeral.

When Mary passed, the insurance paid her total coverage without delay or questions asked. After her passage I asked to work only two days a week, condensing my week hours to two days so I could stay home and write this book. That was graciously granted. Proceeds from Mary's life insurance will be used entirely on this book project so that it will be ready for launch by her first-year anniversary. Thus, the seed from a job that took Mary's faith, patience, persistence, and boldness to get me to take will help put in writing a testimony to how these and other spiritual gifts operated in her and through her life. This is a story that I owe to our children, to our grandchildren, and to generations to come, to family members and to all our friends. It is the story of who she was, what she had, and what she did with what God gave her within the life space He gave her. In a nut shell how Mary loved and served God, loved and faithfully served her husband, adoringly loved her children and grandchildren, loved her family and her friends.

PART 5

PART

CHAPTER 8

A General Who Marched on to the End In Defiance of Infirmities

HER BODY HURT BUT HER SPIRIT WAS ALWAYS STRONG AND ALERT

At times, confusion caused by depression complicated treatment and management of the terminal kidney failure that dominated the last five years of Mary's life on earth. She would spend twelve hours every week sitting in one spot, tethered to a dialysis machine for four long hours at a time. This was unacceptable, deliberate torture in the distorted mind of a person often dealing with depression at the same time. Mary would ask the doctors and nurses treating her, "Why are you torturing me? Why are you punishing me? What have I done?"

She spoke out of physical and mental exhaustion, sometimes not understanding why she had to undergo all these "unnecessary" treatments. Mary would sometimes refuse to go to the clinic for dialysis, no matter how much we tried to persuade her. She would look at me and say, "You always say you love me. Is this really love? To let me go through what I am going through now? How can you truly say that you love me?" Such expressions of desperation left me deeply wounded, frustrated, and helpless at times, knowing that while her body was hurting, her mental perception was completely disconnected from that reality.

Insertion of a fistula into her blood vessel was one of the most difficult operations for me to persuade Mary to endorse. She resisted it every time it came up. This was an unacceptable blemish on her beauty! Mary was a woman of spotless beauty, something I noted from the day I met her in high school. She was without a blemish or a wrinkle on any part of her skin, not even a pimple on her baby face.

Even later in life, Mary's beauty was low maintenance, needing minimum cosmetics to enhance, and that is the way she wanted things to remain forever, no matter what. She would rather have risked the consequences of doing without dialysis, even death itself, than to have protruding objects, visible to the eye, plugged in or protruding from her body. For the same reason, Mary preferred hemodialysis over peritoneal dialysis because the former involved minimal invasion and was less cumbersome and easy to cover.

After access to the bloodstream was created by inserting a fistula into a main blood vein, all that remained was to get regular dialysis at a clinic. A dialysis machine would act as a mechanical kidney, docked onto her bloodstream through the fistula. A fistula was therefore inserted in Mary's left upper arm into a vein by her muscle, and she was always able to cover it under long-sleeved garments so that an observer would hardly notice the bulge. That is the way she retained her beautiful physical shape throughout the five years after insertion of fistula. Mary was known as one of the most beautiful, best-dressed ladies in many clinics she attended. Outsiders would mistake her for one of the nurses, a visitor to the clinic or administrator. She would march into the clinic in her stylish high hills or high ankle boots, dressed in an elegant skirt suit and a beautiful hat and especially when she drove herself and no one could believe she was going to sit on the dialysis chair for the next four hours. By God's grace and goodness, that was the case for five years until the last week of her life when I had to carry her on my back into our car to go for the last dialysis session. Mary refused to be conveyed to clinics by the special public transportation. I had either to drop her or she would drive herself to clinic.

More details on the differences between hemodialysis and peritoneal dialysis can be found at http://www.webmd.com/a-to-z-guides/kidney-dialysis#2.

Mary would allow nothing to slow her down, to make her look unattractive, or for that matter to attract curiosity or sympathies. Mary loved freedom of movement. She was an uninhibited bird and wanted to mix freely with other ministers and with the congregation without looking odd. And despite her infirmities, God granted her desire to the end: to look good, to think good and to act good. At All Nations Church in Irving, Texas, where she had become a regular attendant, she would excitedly participate in a church-organized beauty queen contest with ladies much younger than our daughter Caroline. Mary was beautiful and always generous in affirming others for their beauty and beautiful outfits.

THE GENESIS OF DEPRESSION IN MARY

Mary's depression was triggered by early onset of menopause in 1993. She was about thirty-seven years old and too young. (See details on complications arising from early menopause at http://earlymenopause.com/intro.htm.) Fortunately, thanks to God, she was already a mother of two healthy adolescent children by that time: Caroline was thirteen and Armstrong eleven when menopause occurred.

Treatment of depression involved medications, some of which were still new on the market in the late 1990s. Their side effects had not been fully determined. After having been on Zyprexa (Olanzapine), an antidepressant, on trial, like many other thousands of users, Mary developed diabetes, one of the side effects established after a multistate civil lawsuit in 2007. That led to compensations for thousands of people who had experienced different side effects associated with use of the Zyprexa. The lawsuit even cited cases of deaths. Mary was identified as one of the sufferers of diabetes caused by Zyprexa and became a candidate for compensation.

We did not realize that diabetes, for which she was minimally compensated, would eventually lead to a terminal kidney disease that was diagnosed two years later toward the end of 2009. That condition made her last five years of life the most miserable for her and for her family as we became partakers in her struggles with several health problems. She suffered from depression, diabetes, high blood pressure, and terminal kidney failure.

MINISTRY—A DO-OR-DIE CALLING FOR MARY

None of these conditions or the combination thereof made Mary slowdown in her ministry calling. One time when I was trying to persuade her to cut back her activities with her International Prayer Network ministry, she said, "IPN is me and I am IPN. How can you kill my ministry without killing me? I will give it every resource God has given me, material, time, and energy, until my last breath." From that moment, none of her family members, who were all concerned about her deteriorating health, would stand in her way. And true to her words, she left home on her final week with ministry activity plans fresh on her desk.

Mary never opened her mouth to complain that God had forsaken her. But at the beginning of 2014 she started suffering from a severe backache and was forced to stay in bed most of the day. She could not even go to church or host a Bible study group that used to meet in our apartment. The severity of the pain made her skip dialysis treatment at times. That crippling backache was later diagnosed as coming from gallstones, but the doctors were reluctant to operate, concerned about possible complications.

Finally the pain became unbearable, and Mary insisted that the gallstones be removed at any cost so she would be strong enough, purposely so she would go out and about her work of ministry. Mary's calling to ministry was a do-or-die deal. Concerns for this work came before concerns for her health, no matter how much we tried to get her to slow down. "…I am compelled to preach. Woe to me if I do not preach the gospel!" (1 Corinthians 9:16 NIV).

However, the situation changed dramatically within one week of the operation. The gallstones were removed on May 28, 2014, and I brought Mary home for one night. The following morning after giving her a sponge bath, I had to carry her on my back to the car for a trip to the dialysis clinic. By midnight on May 29, she was in extremely serious condition, and Armstrong helped me to rush her to the emergency room at Baylor Medical Center. Mary showed some improvement over the following week, smiling, teasing, and joking, but she tarried only long enough to enable us to gather as a family to say last good-byes. Caroline flew in from Georgia and camped by her mother's bedside as her system slowly shut down.

That process went on until as late as 2 a.m. on June 4 when I was massaging Mary's neck and back, something she always loved. That would be the last time I talked to her, calling her "my beloved," the title that had replaced her name, and saying "I love you very much" as I departed. Caroline remained at what had become her twenty-four-hour post since her arrival, and by around 3:45 a.m. she was on the phone telling me to come back quickly because "Mom's condition worsened and they had to return her to the ICU."

By the time I got there and Armstrong had joined us and Jerusha soon after, all we could do was sit in the waiting room as the team of doctors and nurses worked hard to keep Mary alive. But at 6:38 a.m. on June 4, 2014, she had a divine appointment with her Lord, alive in the spirit and carrying her sheaves and so absent from us in the flesh. All we had come to do was to escort her and to wave good-bye. She was declared unresponsive by the doctor in charge of a team that worked tirelessly and gallantly trying to keep her alive in the flesh for us.

We all hurt whenever Mary hurt because we loved her and were in this battle together. Over her years of struggling with depression, she remained robust and healthy for as long as she stayed on her minimum dosage of antidepressant. But the moment she would assume that she had healed and secretly discontinued taking the medicine, depression would return subtly, and before we knew it, she was already beyond point the point of voluntary care. It would take involuntary hospitalization and medication to turn her around again. She had at least four major episodes over twenty-one years (1993, 1996, 2001, and 2011) and several minor episodes. They hurt Mary emotionally and caused great distress to her family members who over the years had become so lovingly close to her and dependent on her physically, spiritually, and emotionally. Mary was there for each of us and each of us was there for Mary, it's just amazing!

Our family life and our ministry work would stall during these prolonged periods of depression. We would be cut off from friends whenever Mary was down with depression. Friends would call to visit or to invite us to their functions, but we were in no condition to be visited or to visit. During such episodes no amount of persuasion would make Mary want to go to hospital because she never believed she was suffering from depression.

In the same way she denied suffering from depression, she also vehemently refused to accept the diagnosis of kidney failure that was made toward the end of 2009. According to her, this was a figment of her doctors' imaginations. She did not, therefore, see the necessity for regular kidney dialysis or a regimen of "can eat/drink or can't eat/drink." Such restrictions were irrelevant to her.

Cathy, her first renal dietitian, made a huge mistake one day trying to be tough with Mary on the restrictions. Looking her straight in the eye, she sounded a stern warning as she did to all her patients: "Mary, if you eat the foods on the 'do not eat' list, you will surely die!" Cathy's intention was to scare her patients away from diets that would exacerbate their renal conditions. But Mary, at an early stage of depression and still trying to come to terms with the report on her renal condition, interpreted Cathy's words to mean that she had no hope and was as good as dead.

Mary loved life and believed in life. She never talked of death with reference to herself, no matter how sick she got. Death was not a word Mary was used to hearing, and so for Cathy to use it while looking at Mary in the eye was tantamount to declaring her dead. That did not help their relationship. From that point on, Mary dreaded and resisted meeting Cathy in our weekly team session. That resistance spread to the whole treatment team and eventually to all the clinics in Waco.

Whenever Mary resisted treatment, I resorted to tough love because she was all I had. In 2010 especially, she would use any flimsy excuse to skip dialysis sessions. At times, she would be noncompliant for two to three weeks, and even after fluids and potassium accumulated in her system beyond what any clinic could extract, she would refuse to be taken for emergency care at the main hospital. Her whole body would swell up with fluids like a stuffed sausage to the point that when the adult protective services officer whom I had called to our home in Waco saw her, he immediately called the emergency ambulance team.

When crew members got to our home and tried to persuade Mary to be taken to emergency and she refused, they called in a police patrol, hoping that she could be intimidated. However, she did not care about their presence. The officers, knowing that the law prohibited them from touching her or using any kind of force against her will, resorted to politely trying to persuade her, but she would not bulge. She sat still seeping her cup of coffee and a toast of bread without saying a word.

Finally, the emergency team used a special clause in the regulations. According to the clause, if the team was summoned to attend to an emergency situation as in this case, the person being evacuated would be given a choice to consent to or to decline the service. Either way, the person had to sign the form. If the person were physically disabled, there was an alternative way of signing. But if an abled person like Mary chose not to sign the form and team members determined that the patient was in danger of sudden death, the clause allowed them to evacuate the person against his or her will with all necessary care and precaution.

Mary was physically able but unwilling to sign the form. At that point, on the grounds that Mary was in danger of sudden death, team members read the clause to Mary as if reading her Miranda rights and told her that they would lift her up and help her to the wheelchair unless she was willing to do it herself. The wheelchair converted to a stretcher. She then slowly and reluctantly stood up and sat on the wheelchair. Crew members thanked Mary and converted it to a stretcher. They strapped her in for safety, wheeled her into the waiting ambulance, and whisked her to Providence Hospital emergency room. I followed in my car behind the ambulance, bringing Mary's personal belongings to the hospital since I knew she would be admitted as in times past. I went straight to the receiving bay where she was brought for check-in.

All this drama, which took hours, was painful for me to watch, knowing that if Mary had stayed on one tiny five-milligram pill daily to keep her from depression and so to remain compliant and productive, she would also spare me and the family the distress. *If only she took this little pill faithfully,* I said to myself, *this drama wouldn't keep recurring.* This was a repeat of painful dramas I had been through before. There had been three major episodes before this since 1993 the first time it happened in Springfield, Virginia. But every time I looked at Mary's eyes, I would read innocence because it is not a deliberate choice she makes to discontinue her pill and from that I would feel so much compassion for her.

I always remembered the words of Dr. David, a Christian Psychiatrist who attended her that first time in Springfield: "It is not a deliberate choice Mary makes. These are chemical imbalances in her brains beyond her control. She thinks she is healed and doesn't need the pill anymore. She means well, but it doesn't always end well unless she has caring support from medics, friends, and a loving family. It takes tough and tender love." This doctor laid a sure foundation on which I would remain strong for my beloved wife for decades. I showed tough love by involving assertive care teams whenever necessary to bring Mary to where she could get help even though this was always against her will and she was occasionally in tears, something I hated to see in Mary's eyes. (In forty years of friendship and marriage, Mary never shed a tear because of anything I did or said to her.)

Doctor David also told me to treat Mary with respect and tender love after her recovery and not to put her on a guilt trip for having decided to discontinue taking her antidepressants. This was not a choice such patients always make consciously. He told me, "You have to monitor her indirectly and ensure regular refills and not depend on her to do it." He shared with me his personal experience with fighting depression.

Any time my wife discontinued taking her antidepressants, I was partly to blame because I had also become complacent and overconfident about her self-management. We would be so busy doing great ministry work together and going about life's activities that I would slack off in monitoring her and she wouldn't take her regular dosage. Then depression would slowly overtake her, and before we realized it, she was already at a point of no return and soon on the deep end.

DENIED DIALYSIS BY DOCTORS IN WACO FOR NONCOMPLIANCE

Back to the emergency room at Providence where she was brought against her will. Mary refused to communicate with doctors or nurses and as in times past, it was my duty to provide all the necessary information so she could be admitted. Eventually, after her treatment began, doctors used the opportunity to combine her antidepressant medication with kidney dialysis treatment, addressing both problems at the same time intravenously. Mary would soon start cooperating with kidney treatment. But after several episodes in which Mary refused to cooperate and risked her life, the dialysis doctors in Waco became frustrated and decided they could not continue treating her against her will. They signed a document saying that based on her noncompliance, they would exercise their right to choose not to treat her in the future.

I was stunned to hear that, and calling to mind Doctor David's words, I wondered why these doctors would be so indifferent, inhumane, and insensitive to my wife's predicaments. Why did they view her condition as a deliberate choice? I tried to argue with the doctors, citing Mary's incompetence when depressed, but they countered my argument by invoking the Texas law that gives doctors the liberty to choose not to treat patients against their will regardless of their mental state. According to the same law, it was her sovereign right to decline treatment offered to her, and so they were not allowed to force it on her and neither could we as family. With that, my argument lost steam, and I asked them what other options were open to us. Still placing the responsibility on her, the lead doctor said that Mary had the right to choose any option she felt more comfortable with, including moving to a new area or choosing hospice, especially being a terminal case. Since we were not sure what hospice services entailed, this was explained to her.

At the end of this round of treatment, Mary signed her own release from the hospital. She was furnished with a copy of the signed statement by the doctors, meaning that unless she relocated, her only option was hospice service, on condition she signed up for it. That meant she would no longer receive further kidney treatment or medication in Waco under any circumstances and instead would have to depend on basic comforts from any excessive pain as provided by hospice services until she died at her home or at a hospice facility. To my surprise, Mary accepted the terms, and with that understanding, the doctors released her from the hospital.

This development was traumatic to our family, forcing Caroline and her family to travel all the way back to Waco from Atlanta so all of us could spend time together for what seemed like the final time unless Mary would let us try other options. We could not wait until she started accumulating fluids and potassium in her body again. No sooner had Mary arrived home when the hospice team came knocking at our door to explain the services further and to get Mary to sign up. However, we did not know that Mary had changed her mind about hospice services. She declined to sign the necessary forms. By that time, her body had once again started showing signs of swelling from fluids. We were racing against time.

RACING AGAINST TIME—PLAN B AS A BRIDGE TO GEORGIA

We started working on plans B and C. Under plan B, we sought clinics outside Waco where I could shuttle Mary on a temporary basis as a bridge to plan C. As we searched, God opened a clinic in Temple about a forty-five-minute drive south of Waco. This was great news even to Mary, but this was only a bridge to plan C—to relocate Mary to Georgia with Caroline's family on a longer but still temporary basis. We believed that a change of scenery and treatment team while in Georgia would give Mary a fresh beginning and thus another chance. Also, being with the Daughter's family, especially her granddaughter, would have a positive impact and give her new motivation.

The moment the family brought this proposal to the table, Mary started packing for Georgia, and just as expected, she hit the ground running once there, not only making new friends among her treatment team but also doing ministry work through her International Prayer Network. Mary blended in very well with her daughter's family. She gained weight, had a change of demeanor, and got a fresh burst of energy seen only many years before. She was able to keep up with her granddaughter's pace and to support the family just like any other robustly healthy grandmother. She would cook creative meals and participate in all family functions in addition to doing her occasional prayer meetings and attending activities of ministries in the area.

These things occupied most of her time in Georgia from around June 2010 to January 2011. I was so impressed with her improvement that I started thinking of selling our home in Waco and relocating to Georgia for Mary's sake. To gain a feel for Georgia and the opportunities there, I joined her for a couple of months toward the end of the year. We were now both guests of Caroline's family, but in January 2011, Mary started missing Texas and asked if we could move back. However, since she could not get treatment in Waco, Mary suggested that she move to the Irving area and stay in a hotel from where she could get treatment at a nearby dialysis clinic and participate as a prayer partner in the Benny Hinn Ministry based in Grapevine. I would visit with her on weekends.

I had no problem with that because Mary was driving herself in her beautiful Chevy Lumina four-door with her International Prayer Network logo and own color photo emblazoned on the side. She was all set and comfortable in her ensuite at the DFW Hotel. In the meantime, we would look for a buyer for our mansion in Waco and permanently relocate to the Irving or Grapevine areas in Texas. My love for Mary and my desire for her wellness and comfort superseded anything else that was dear to me. I always struggled to say no to Mary's requests, especially in her years of health struggles with kidney failure. Just as in Georgia, I was ready to sell our mansion at a throwaway price to meet Mary's desire to move to Irving. Since my job was in Waco, I visited her only on weekends, spending time together in the hotel where she was now a resident. She even held a prayer meeting there.

This arrangement continued for most of February to May, but all was not well, and the problem became fully manifest in June 2011. Mary had become overconfident again about her wellness and had quietly stopped taking her daily dosage of antidepressants, especially because I was not there to keep track of her daily intake and regular refills. From past experiences, I had started noticing the telltale signs and decided to keep observing. But soon after, I started getting calls from her dialysis clinic asking why Mary was missing treatments. That alarmed me and I decided to check with her. She told me of having problems with the car. I asked why she did not let me know sooner so I could call our ministry partners to convey her for treatment. When she wouldn't communicate further, I sensed trouble.

Alarmed by that and by the nurses' reports, Armstrong and I decided to stay with her at the hotel over the weekend because she was always deeply attached to our son and would listen to and communicate with him even at the lowest point in her depression when she would not communicate with anybody else. As always, Mary chose ministry work above every other activity including treatment and would often get too busy to the point of forgetting her antidepressant dosage or her refill. The signs were now clear that this is what she had done.

We decided that the three of us would spend the whole day together so Armstrong and I could persuade her to resume her dosage and to get back on dialysis, but by now she had reached a point of no return. Nothing could persuade her or motivate her including the wedding of Armstrong and Jerusha in one month's time, an event we hoped could stimulate her mind.

We were wrong. Mary was already fully into her own world of realities from where no other reality existed. Worse still, she was not eating properly and spent most of the day and night locked in her hotel room covered from head to toe. A family friend who frequently alternated visits with me would go out to lunch with Mary, but now my wife would not allow her into the room. The staff had also started noticing that Mary looked sickly. She would sign for services without scrutinizing them, so they devised a way of siphoning her money by fraudulently charging her bank card. We discovered this later and took action against the hotel to recover every penny the staff had stolen to the tune of $3,500.

After that long weekend we spent with her, we fully established that Mary was down and under. We decided it was time to take action in line with what we had learned to do in situations like this before. The most loved, adored, and jealously protected member of the Nkoyo family had to be hospitalized involuntarily for treatment of depression and for resumption of dialysis treatment. The danger to her life from skipping kidney treatment was our strongest justification for involuntary admission and treatment. Poor eating habits had also caused Mary to lose weight to a dangerous level. That is what we stated as the reason for requesting her involuntary admission. By afternoon of the same day we reported her situation, an agency specialized in handling that kind of patient came to the hotel to pick her and take her to Parkland Medical Center in Dallas for treatment of depression and for kidney dialysis.

THE LONGEST HOSPITALIZATION IN MARY'S STRUGGLE WITH DEPRESSION

Mary remained in Parkland Hospital for three moths long after she had recovered. The hospital could not release her until a dialysis clinic in the Dallas, Waco, or Temple areas was willing to treat her, but none would at that time, based on her well-known record of noncompliance. Dialysis clinics are commercial entities contracted by the government to treat Medicare-Medicaid patients and others. Dialysis seats are assigned to patients, and if a patient fails to show up without calling in advance and the seat isn't reallocated, the clinic loses money. Thus noncompliant patients are viewed as economic liabilities. Unfortunately, Mary's history of noncompliance made her a liability, and any clinic compassionate enough to open its doors to her did so at its own economic risk. With that history, Mary was stuck at Parkland for a while. Eventually, she had to return to Georgia, again staying with our daughter's family while dialyzing there in a clinic where her status was still intact. She remained there until August 2012 when an opportunity opened again in Irving, Texas. The details of that dramatic move and the miraculous events leading to our eventual relocation to Irving were described earlier in this book.

For twenty-one years, Mary suffered from a buildup of conditions, starting with depression, triggered by a biological clock that lost steam too early. And as with many others, who struggle with depression, her mind was in constant denial, not by choice, but by the subtle nature of this infirmity. However, Mary's spirit remained strong, alive, and alert to the promptings of the Holy Spirit, always placing the first thing first. "But seek first the kingdom of God and His righteousness, and all these things shall be added to you" (Matthew 6:33 NKJV).

Mary kept a busy schedule as a seeker of the kingdom and helping others find it. That is why I loved her and did whatever God put in my power to do to keep her standing to fight the good fight of faith. I never abandoned her in those moments she was down and under, because those were the times when she needed me most. That became my driving purpose. Her loving family became "all things added to her."

A WOUNDED WARRIOR WHO NEVER FALTERED OR FAINTED - BIBLICAL PARALLELS

In the Old Testament, we read the story of a revered and decorated general who was also a leper. "Now Naaman, commander of the army of the king of Syria, was a great and honorable man in the eyes of his master, because by him the Lord had given victory to Syria. He was also a mighty man of valor, but a leper" (2 Kings 5:1).

Knowing what leprosy does to human limbs, and having served as an officer all my twelve years in the military, I often wonder how general Naaman functioned while serving at the top rank in the Syrian army. Even though as a general he did not have to duel with a sword or throw a javelin, I am still at a loss as to how he stood before his subordinate commanders and gave operational orders as a leper. But this is the man to whom the king of Syria had entrusted all matters of national security. In that introductory verse, we are told that Naaman performed honorably, never faltering or giving retreat orders to his army. But in the same verse we are told of the invisible and invincible force that was always behind the man despite his infirmities and why he became a success: "by him the Lord had given victory to Syria."

One is left wondering why God would choose to stand behind a man with leprosy, a sign of weakness, and through him to bring victory to a nation. Why would He bypass so many strong and good-looking officers as in the story of how He chose the boy David? We may never know the whole story, but in another Scripture verse we get an idea. "But God hath chosen the foolish things of the world to confound the wise; and God hath chosen the weak things of the world to confound the things which are mighty" (1 Corinthians 1:27 KJV).

When the apostle Paul wrote this in his first letter to the Corinthians, one wonders whether he had his own infirmities in mind when talking about weak things because in his second letter to the same believer he specifically referred to himself, saying, "Because of the surpassing greatness of the revelations, for this reason, to keep me from exalting myself, there was given me a thorn in the flesh, a messenger of Satan to torment me—to keep me from exalting myself. Concerning this I implored the Lord three times that it might leave me" (2 Corinthians 12:7–8).

Reading these two verses by Paul discussing his prowess in revelation and yet his fleshly infirmities, I am always able to relate to Mary's infirmities. That is because no one understood the greatness of anointing that flowed through her in terms of prophetic pronouncements, word of knowledge, and faith more than I did, having been by her side for forty years, and neither is there anyone who understands the depth of her sufferings better than I do, having been a partaker in them for the last twenty-one years of her life. Whether this was for the same purpose as in Paul's case, to keep

Mary from exalting herself, I may never know, but one thing I do know: Mary never sought sympathy from anyone and never complained to her Master about her sufferings. Mary may have been wounded while on the battlefield, but she remained defiant; she may have been outgunned and outnumbered and had to stand alone at times, but she remained daring and steadfast to her last breath, holding up the candle of her International Prayer Network ministry and keeping it burning to the end.

Like Syria in Naaman's time, our family and innumerable others became beneficiaries of victory after victory with God working behind the scenes and through Mary, dating back to 1974 when as a youth she prayed for that crippled boy in my hometown market and started walking, prayed for the salvation of my father, my older sister, and my uncle among many others and led them to Christ in the first largest crusade my people had witnessed. And despite her struggles with depression and kidney failure toward the end, Mary's courage, boldness, and faith opened innumerable doors to opportunities and foiled the Enemy's grand plans to steal from, to kill, and to destroy her family. All the way to her last breath she remained true to her calling in the work of ministry because even when she was weak in the flesh, she was strong in the Spirit.

We heard her voice asking her Master for rest and witnessed her triumphal entry into His glory when in her last words to Caroline she spoke softly and without bitterness or stress, saying, "I am tired. I need to rest." And on the day when we laid her to rest, our family did not have to walk alone, but was shoulder to shoulder with hundreds of friends whom Mary had made because she was friendly. With these friends we joined to celebrate a life well lived by Mary as if to affirm her famous attitude of faith in God even when it made no sense. This was summed up in her own words: "Even if He chooses not to deliver me from this suffering body, He is still able and worthy of my service and praise."

Epilogue

A tribute to a hero, the Rev. Mary Muthoni Nkoyo, a general who never faltered, feared, or fainted in the face of fierce enemy fire
(ENLISTED, 1973; PROMOTED TO GLORY, JUNE 4, 2014)

Mary must be remembered for generations by the Nkoyo family and members of the household of faith as a warrior who from a prostrate position kept her finger on the trigger and her sights trained on a fierce enemy. Wounded and yet defiant, outgunned, and outnumbered, she refused to surrender until her last breath. Like the Hebrew children faced with a fiery furnace, she defied the enemy, saying, "Even if God chooses not to deliver me from this suffering body, He is still able and worthy of my service and praise. He called me to stand in the gap, even when I have to stand alone."

With a defiant faith that made no sense to the world, Mary opened doors for her family to prosper, held the family's enemies at bay, and kept the ministry candle aflame to the end.

Foregoing is a true account of the acts and times of Rev. Mary Nkoyo by written by Reverend Wilfred Nkoyo (Major Retired) her loving husband of thirty-five years and best friend of forty years. His major role toward the end of this warrior's life on earth was to provide spiritual, material and moral support on the battlefield. Whenever the warrior lay wounded on the ground, he reached out and raised her up so she could continue the fight and keep the enemy pinned down. He was by her side to the moment of her promotion to glory on June 4, 2014. And finally, on June 14, 2014, in the company of other saints who turned up to give her the final salute and honors befitting a decorated general who gallantly fought the good fight and won tough battles for the glory of King of Kings.

Appendix

Family Friends and Their Testimonies About the Nkoyo Family and Salutations to Rev. Mary Nkoyo

DR. SAMMY AND DR. MARY MURIMI

Writing this is not easy, because years of memories come flooding back. I knew our late sister when she was a young student at Nyandarua High School. The Lord gave me the privilege not only of witnessing her accept Him in high school but of walking that new life with her until her translation to heaven. I was one of the maids in her wedding, an invitation that reflected acceptance into the new family's inner circle.

The path that our brother Wilfred and sister Mary took is extraordinary and remarkable! They started their journey young, but they were powerhouses of vision, ambition, and unparalleled drive. Both visualized things twenty years ago that some of us are just starting to contemplate. Their dreams would awe those who did not understand these visions. Unlike most couples, with one a leader and the other a follower, Mary and Wilfred were both leaders and followers, and therefore led and followed each other throughout their journey. As forward-thinking leaders, they took risks; some came back to bite them, and some elevated their visions and made them the people they truly were. For the Nkoyos, fear was not a factor, and numbers did not matter when it came to carrying out their mission. That was because they were grounded in the Word and depended on God. Their prayer life was unsurpassed!

As a result, when the storms started raging (and they sure did!), the two were like a tree planted by the water's side. They cheated the Devil through strong prayers and godly parenting, especially when storms blew by their children. Their two children are models today despite the storms during their teenage years. And when financial storms came along, they only left the Nkoyos in a better financial situation!

The Nkoyos cheated death when the storm of sickness blew by their family. They chose to hold on to hope and move forward. This storm had the potential of destroying their union, but the Lord had erected strong walls made of love, commitment, and prayers.

The one word I can use to describe this family is *resilience.*

My dear sister and friend, my daughter in faith Mary, was still organizing marriage and prayer seminars even in the last month of her life here on earth despite so much pain and physical weakness. She did what the Lord Jesus told her to do even if only two people would attend the seminars.

Mary and Wilfred invited me to speak at many of their seminars, but time conflicts would never allow that. I look forward to attending and speaking at marriage seminars arranged in her honor in the future.

Mary Murimi, Ph.D., RD., is professor of nutrition at the Texas Tech University College of Human Sciences in Lubbock, Texas, and vice president of the Society for Nutrition Education and Behavior. Her husband, Sammy Murimi, D.Min., is the director of Share International, Inc. They have been married for thirty-two years.

REV. AYUB AND REV. ANNE MUTHAMA

Eternal life is one thing that Mary was always very sure of. "Jesus Christ gives eternal life to all those who believe in Him," she proclaimed. Jesus is God eternal, and He gives the same to all who believe in Him that they too by faith may manifest the life of God in their mortal bodies. That in a nutshell was Mary's position of faith, one by which she lived throughout the time I knew her, going back to our days as working single girls sharing an apartment in Nairobi, Kenya. In those days, we used to go out on preaching missions on the weekends and would get so excited when we saw high school girls respond in tears as we invited them to give their lives to Jesus. Our motto was "Kitchens Beyond," because we believed that our ministry calling was beyond a life of cooking in the kitchen.

My husband, the Rev. Ayub Muthama, and I, now married for thirty-four years, remained in constant fellowship with the Revs. Wilfred and Mary Nkoyo. They were one year ahead of us in marriage, and I had the unique privilege of participating in their colorful military wedding as one of the bridesmaids. The ceremony was held in Narok, Kenya, their hometown. As couples and parents, we shared lots of fun about our marriage experiences and parenting. Mary loved families and she always talked about how to plan couples' retreats, an effort in which she was very involved. When I became the vice president of the Kenya Christian Fellowship in America and decided to hold its first women's conference, I invited the Rev. Mary Nkoyo as our first speaker. She was such a blessing. A powerful speaker under great anointing, she presented the gospel with simplicity and great humor that made it come alive.

We also had somber moments, moments of weeping and praying together during tough times occasioned by Mary's ill health. Over a prolonged time, while in the United States, Mary struggled with depression a condition which was effectively controlled through antidepressants. But, whenever she withdrew from her pill and conditions were bad, her loving husband would invite us to be there to give her and the family moral support based on our past relationship as single girls. I often felt very sad and helpless because all I could do was pray for her and her family during such episodes. I could not persuade her to resume her prescriptions or go to hospital for treatment, because like many patients dealing with depression she struggled with denial. Prayer remained our most effectual weapon in helping Mary overcome these periodic attacks of depression and also of kidney disease, which she suffered in her last five years of life. We thank God so much because He answers prayers.

Words fail us concerning the Reverend Nkoyo, Mary's husband. He is truly a hero. He remained faithful and steadfast, always passionately loving his wife and supporting her even when she was withdrawn and would not talk to him for many months. He rallied his children around their mother, and as a family, they stood together shoulder to shoulder (son-in-law and daughter-in-law included) to the very end, carrying the remains of their beloved to her final resting place as the whole world watched in amazement. What an example of the love of Christ for the church! Many marriages will be healed and enhanced as couples read the true love story of Mary and Wilfred and about their focused children and the Nkoyos' faith in Christ their Savior.

The Reverend Ayub and I will forever be grateful to have known and been friends with such a wonderful couple and family and to God for allowing us to share in their lives during their moments of joy and during their moments of struggle with health and finally in their grief when Mary departed.

DR. JAMES AND MRS. MARGRET NJOROGE

We have known our dear friends the Rev. Maj. Wilfred Nkoyo and his late wife, the Rev. Mary Nkoyo, for more than thirty years. For many years our home in Kenya was their stopover when they travelled from their home in Narok to Nairobi. We served together in the formation of a ministry to couples and families under the Kenya Christian Family Fellowship. The KCFF is still very strong in Kenya, currently under the leadership of couples who were little kids accompanying their parents during KCFF retreats and seminars in the early days. In the United States, the Nkoyo family and our family continued in our friendship, fellowship, and partnership in ministry.

Our late sister Rev. Mary Nkoyo provided passionate leadership of her own ministry, International Prayer Network, until her last breath. This ministry, which regularly called Christians together to pray, met in hotel ballrooms and lobbies. Members prayed for families and nations and had an impact on many couples and families across the globe. Many today will testify that they owe the strength of their marriage commitment and their parenting success to the Nkoyos' ministry. This couple had a passion to help others succeed in these two aspects.

The strength of our marriage commitment and our success as parents of three now-independent young adults stems in large part from our association with the Nkoyo family. Citing one example, while living in Virginia in 2008, we sensed vulnerability to the stability and success of our sixteen-year-old son. We did the best we could as his loving parents, but his response was unimpressive, so we called upon the Nkoyos in Waco, Texas, to see if they could take him in for a change of social influence and apply their superior skills in handling youths in crisis to help refocus him. We also wanted their twenty-six-year-old son Armstrong to help in positive role modeling.

They teamed up and readily accepted our son into their family and for three years cared for him in their home as one of their own. He responded excellently to their love and guidance, resuming work on his high school diploma, which he had abandoned just six months before graduation, and going on to the Texas State Technical College in Waco, a nationally known technical college that Armstrong had attended. Our reformed son turned into a great asset, respectful and dependable, always referring to Mary as "Mom" and to Major Nkoyo as "uncle." Today, back in Virginia, he is an independent, law-abiding citizen and a successful automotive mechanic. Today, he is our great pride and a role model to others.

This book is not only a tribute to the Reverend Mary as an effective minister of the gospel, a faithful and loving wife, and a loving mother, but a document that addresses issues of marriage commitment and parenting, both critical to success in family life. My wife and I can attest to the fact that there are no perfect marriages. After all, there are no perfect people, not even the Nkoyos. However, the Nkoyos' fire-tested relationship resulted in a strong marriage commitment, and they developed unique parenting skills, providing a model in critical aspects of family life. This was visible in two ways. First, the Reverend Nkoyo continued to support and remain lovingly committed to his wife during the darkest moments in her twenty-one years of on-and-off struggles with depression and eventually with terminal kidney disease. Sad to say, in such circumstances many find a reason to abandon their spouse and run for greener pastures. Second, he rallied his children to the same course and kept them focused on their development, turning them into the success stories they are today with independent families of their own. These highly commendable accomplishments and perfect examples glorify God and provide great encouragement to the household of faith.

The concept of indebtedness to other entities in a commitment to one's spouse sounds like a new approach to marriage relationships, but in truth this concept is part of many cultures and religions. However, we have given little attention to this idea, which the author fully exposes and exemplifies. This thought-provoking challenge calls upon the reader to recognize those entities working behind the scenes in our marriage relationships, which if given preeminence will enhance our marriage commitment, giving it a solid purpose and the power to surmount any difficulties in life.

This book will be an effective tool for dealing with issues that affect couples and families in Africa and elsewhere in the world who still believe in marriage as an act of God that brings one woman and one man into union as one entity separable only by death. The book's wealth of wisdom, practical experience, and biblical lessons will be helpful to couples and families seeking to overcome critical challenges concerning marriage and parenting. The author is a man of God who lives, leads, and serves others by example and who follows the principles shared in this book. He and his late wife built a closely knit family, bound with the cords of love and respect. As a family, the Nkoyos genuinely love their brethren, and as a couple, they were passionate about strong and stable marriage commitments and positive parenting. Mary and Wilfred never practiced "helicopter" parenting, but at great sacrifice of material gain, were always available to their children and, recently, to their grandchildren. They are a great example to couples with children and grandchildren.

Singles in serious courtship, married couples, and those parenting should read this book if they want to discover the external entities to which they owe a marriage commitment. In so doing, they will find a purpose that will become the driving force in their relationship. We are glad to endorse this book.

Dr. James Njoroge is an affiliate pastor of Crossroads Presbyterian Church, a member of the KCFF Board of Trustees, director of David Hope International, of Jamii International Outreach Ministries, and of Hope for the Nations International. He and his wife Margret live in northern Virginia in the United States and have been married for thirty-four years.

REV. DR. JOSEPH AND REV. MARGRET NJOROGE

How delightful it is for us to commend Maj. Wilfred Nkoyo's tribute to his wife and our dear friend, the Rev. Mary Nkoyo. We knew Mary since our youth in the early '70s and can attest to the enduring nature of their relationship from their wedding, which we attended in October 1979, until the Lord called Mary to our eternal home. Mary knew the weapon of a Christian's warfare. She never got tired of calling the body of Christ to prayer and therefore launched her ministry, the International Prayer Network, based in her family home in Waco, Texas, in a ceremony at which we were privileged to officiate in 2010.

She lived boldly, professing like the apostle Paul, "For me to live is Christ and to die is gain." Even during the most difficult times of her life, she would call all her friends for prayer—not to pray for her, but to pray for concerns that are important in families and to the nation's life. She also made telephone calls and asked, "How is your son?" or "How is your daughter?" She was not satisfied with hearing that a child was fine. She would delve deeper and say, "Tell me how your child is doing at work, at school, or in general." This was how Mary demonstrated her caring character.

She walked faithfully and confidently in her ministry, showing great strength in some of the most difficult times. This was revealed when her family had to return to Kenya from the United States in May 1984 after her husband was abruptly recalled from his diplomatic post in Washington, D.C. She had the opportunity to stay in the United States with her children and all the family's material belongings and continue her education at the University of the District of Columbia. During this time, before the era of the rotary green card, individuals who came to the United States had one primary focus: to pursue education. But Mary would not allow any earthly assignment or call to separate her from her husband and the father of her children. She returned home with their children and joined him, uncertain of his fate.

My husband and I discussed how devastating it was for families that remained in the United States and sacrificed the most valuable relationships to pursue education or money. Looking back, we can say with confidence that Mary chose what was important—family first. The joy of having her family close by her side was her strength. As a wife and a mother myself, I witnessed that in all our discussions during my visit to comfort her on behalf of my family at that time of uncertainty. Within the Kenya diaspora community in America, her character was something to be admired, especially when we consider the many families broken because of long-distance relationships, or commuter marriages. It is nearly impossible to maintain a commuter marriage between Africa and the United States! Confronted with a tough decision, Mary realized her family was her primary responsibility. This was highly commendable.

Mary was a loving person, and this was clear in her relationship with a close friend. Before she got married, we used to meet and pray in Kabete as members of a ladies fellowship. We launched this fellowship to develop close relationships of trust and especially to seek God concerning our future, our spouses-to-be, and by faith the children who would be born out of these faithful relationships. Our circle of friends was blessed by the Lord, and through faith most of us married God-fearing men. The majority of us immigrated to the United States in the 1980s.

Mary knew where each of us had settled and, with her family, made efforts to visit us. Her desire was to bring together the couples in her circle with their families so that the children could meet and build trust with each other the way we as their parents had done. Mary's love for people brought a handful of us together in Waco in the summer of 2010 for a mini retreat. She had passion for families and had prepared her home with this in mind. Several families could come together for a retreat in a friendly home environment and would relax and reconnect. Sometimes we wondered why as friends we lived in different cities. Mary concluded that we were like pioneers in the United States and that God had to scatter us because everywhere each member of our circle of friends lived a fellowship had been launched.

Her daughter Caroline has some of these great qualities. You know a parent is successful when an adult child sounds like the parent! Mary succeeded in transmitting her caring character to her daughter. Through these enduring traits, the essence of Mary will live beyond her earthly life.

This tribute is a reflection of a life well lived within the context of the family, the center stage of the community of faith, and the community at large. In these contexts spouses are called to practice what they believe to be true. Nkoyo's tribute affirms the reality of being married into a spouse's family and of the relationship dynamics surrounding the couple as opposed to being married to just one individual. This testifies to the truth of Hebrews 12:1, which says that a Christian couple is surrounded by a cloud of great witnesses and therefore has responsibility toward each other beyond the confines of their home.

In a day when spouses in bad health are often abandoned and the marriage commitment is shunned by many, this tribute reinforces the vow a couple makes before God to one another, "Till death do us part," and elevates the institution of marriage as honorable before God. This returns marriage to center stage. Indeed, the responsibility for each other applies "in good or in bad times, in sickness or in health," because marriage vows are held together not just by romantic love which fades or by fleeting material considerations, but by an enduring commitment— first to God, second to one another, third to children, and fourth to communities. A sense of indebtedness in our marriage commitment to these and similar entities that we hold dear helps to give purpose to our marriage relationship. This book is more than a tribute. It will make good reading for couples who wish to develop their relationship beyond the superficial level and to venture into deeper, purposeful understanding. It will go further and challenge readers to examine the realities of their marital relationships. When all is said and done, can a spouse say, "I did my best with what was given to me"?

Rev. Wambui Njoroge, M. Sci. (Child and Family Studies),
CEO/Triumph Christian Ministries Inc.
Dr. Joe Njoroge, Ph.D.,
Professor of Political Science and Religion,
President, Triumph Christian Ministries Inc.
(The two are co-founders of Marriage Dynamics National Forum.)

MR. DUNCAN AND MRS. ASENATH GICHIA

My wife Asenath and I have known the Nkoyos for close to thirty-seven years. We met Wilfred in 1977 after we moved to the town of Narok where I was posted to teach at the Narok secondary school. Asenath worked as a nurse in the Narok district hospital. Wilfred had just graduated from the military college and was a commissioned officer in the Kenyan army based in the Gilgil barracks. In Narok, our family joined the Pentecostal Assemblies of God church of which Wilfred was already an active member, very involved in Sunday school and youth activities and often joining the fellowship whenever he visited his hometown. His parents were also active members. We met at this church and became great friends.

With time, we were introduced to Miss Mary Mbuthuri, who occasionally accompanied Wilfred visiting the family. Wilfred and Mary were in courtship going back to 1974 while in high school together, and at that stage the church family had already embraced the relationship based on its openness and their participation in the fellowship. The couple had set an unprecedented example of maturity and purity, and the parents from both sides were very excited and desired to see the couple married. The couple decided to adopt Asenath and me as their role models and to have us counsel them through the final stages toward marriage. Mary chose Asenath to be her maid of honor, and Mary and Wilfred asked me to be their master of ceremonies.

By October 1979, the couple was ready and got married in our local church in a unique and very colorful military ceremony, the first of its kind in Narok. From that event thirty-five years ago, our friendship and fellowship as couples and families grew from strength to strength, with the Nkoyos becoming mentors to our married children. We often got together to celebrate our marriages, our children, and our ministries. Even after we all relocated from Narok, we still found time to get together. In 2009, we travelled to the United States and visited the Nkoyos in Waco, Texas.

The Nkoyos have been our inner-core friends. Our friendship is far deeper than that with our blood brothers and sisters because in them as individuals and as a couple we found genuine love for God and agape (God loving us through them). They became family, their parents our parents and vice versa. Mary's departure is a loss to us all as her loving family, but according to Scripture, it is a gain for her as she has gone to a better place where she will suffer no more after years of physical trials. We mourn her with hope.

The Nkoyos were a living epistle of excellence, showing how a husband can truly love his wife in sickness and in health and how a woman can faithfully love her husband and humble herself before him. They were exemplary in their parenting in tough times and in a challenging environment, America. This book is only a printed record of what was lived out in deed and witnessed by those of us who were there from day one. And now it is up to each one of us to choose to emulate the example set by this couple who walked the talk and ran the race before our eyes.

—Mr. Duncan and Mrs. Asenath Gichia (Juja, Nairobi, Kenya)

BRIG. (RETIRED) PHILLIP AND MRS. MARTHA CHEBBET

It is with much pleasure that my wife Martha and I write about Maj. (Retired) Wilfred Nkoyo and his late wife, our sister in the Lord, the Rev. Mary Nkoyo. I was among the first few to learn about Mary's passing and made a long- distance call from Kenya to Texas to Wilfred and his family to offer a word of comfort.

Wilfred came to Gilgil in April 1977 after his commission in the armed forces as a second lieutenant and was posted to the Kenyan army artillery regiment. I was then a captain, serving with the light armor regiment in the same brigade with him. Two special things bringing us together in friendship and fellowship that have transcended our years in the military were our common faith as Christians and our long-term commitment to our marriages. In both of these, we supported each other right from the beginning.

Wilfred as a professing Christian needed a role model in a Christian officer who had already crystalized, professing his faith openly, first as a Christian and second as a military officer, and he found that in me. When the time came to marry Mary, a dear friend of my fiancée, Martha (whom I would soon marry with the Nkoyos' reciprocating participation), he needed a Christian officer to be his best man and found that in me. These two events were central to the rest of Wilfred's success in the military as a Christian officer and as a man in a marriage that would glorify God. I thank God for giving me both privileges.

Mary and Wilfred opened their home as a meeting place for the Military Christian Fellowship (MCF), alternating with our family. Over the years, Wilfred served on the committee that administered MCF activities in Kenya, and the Nkoyos travelled overseas to represent the organization, especially when they served as diplomats in Washington, D.C.

Any book written as a tribute to the life and work of our sister's ministry would be incomplete if her tremendous and lasting contribution to the women's ministry in the MCF went unmentioned. Mary adapted fully to the military family and even more important, found a mission field among women to which she applied herself with a passion, fully and ably. Her husband became an equally strong leader in an organization that kept the light of Christ shining in the armed forces, serving side by side with those of us who pioneered the work.

To all and sundry, my wife and I bear testimony to the exemplary life lived by the Nkoyos as a Christian couple during our service together and after their retirement. One high point marking our marriages is that as Mary struggled with bouts of depression in her later years and when Martha, my beloved wife, was almost crippled in a near-fatal car accident, we stuck with our spouses because we were committed to doing what godly men must do when their spouses need them most.

—Brig. (Retired) Phillip and Mrs. Martha Chebbet (Nakuru, Kenya)

PASTORS RONNIE AND KIM HOLMES

We are writing this from both a pastoral and a friendship perspective, having known the Nkoyos since 2001. We have watched this husband faithfully support his precious wife's endeavors when she was doing well and still consistently love and care for her during the more challenging times. Thank you for modeling true covenant to us!

Pastors Ronnie and Kim Holmes,
Church of the Open Door
Waco, Texas

DR. WILSON AND MRS. ELIZABETH WAMANI

What a privilege for me and my wife Elizabeth as a couple and as a family, to have known the Nkoyos for more than fourteen years (2001 to 2014) and to have had an opportunity in such an important treatise and tribute to express our love and good memories of the Rev. Mary Nkoyo. She was a confidante and a close friend to us, and my wife and our daughters shared life stories with her freely and sincerely. Memories of this best friend will endure in all our family life stories.

Time and struggles with health drew wrinkles on her fair face, but her fresh colors as a friend and a dear sister in the Lord were such that neither heat, nor cold, nor ill health, nor place, nor destiny, can alter or diminish what she deposited in our memories. Her persona radiated honor, wisdom, integrity, creativity, boldness, and determination to live in peace with friend and foe alike. Mary loved to give and to forgive. She was caring, virtuous, motherly, wifely, and a godly woman.

Like time, which is perhaps our most precious commodity, Mary was precious to all of us. However, unlike time, which once it passes is forever lost, Mary is still with us. My family bears witness that the Rev. Wilfred Nkoyo was highly favored to find and to share life with somebody so faithfully loving. He could not love and value any treasure more than his late wife Mary. We have not found a comparison to what we witnessed in the love dynamics of this couple. Love is measured not just when everything is merry but in how it fares after passing through life's fiery furnaces. My family had the unique privilege of witnessing each stage— the highest moments, the lowest moments, and the times after the fires— and we can report that in the end, Jesus was glorified through love that endured the fire and through a commitment that remained unshakable.

For the glory of God and for the benefit of many couples in the body of Christ, we have shared a fire that the Nkoyos occasionally endured. This is a fire that has in the past and continues today to break many marriages. The Rev. Mary Nkoyo suffered depression attacks that often halted the family's progress for prolonged periods as she lay in the house, sometimes in excess of one year at a time. But the wonder of it all is how her husband would show his adoring love for Mary and would so tenderly pay so much attention to her at the expense of social engagements just like a parent with a suffering child. In moments like these, he would rally his young children to the care of their mother. They united as a family to care for one of their own and did so to the end.

In this regard alone, the Reverend Major Nkoyo exemplified a true marriage commitment to a spouse in sickness and in health to those of us who have been married for many years and have been spared the pain of such fires and to younger couples with uncertain futures. His unshakable stand painted a portrait of a godly husband and a father to his children at a time when many faced with similar or lesser challenges might choose to run and to abandon their families. He did so in words and in deeds. We all witnessed an enduring example of commitment to a marriage.

—Dr. Wilson Wamani (Round Rock, Texas, USA)

REV. PHILIP AND REV. REBECCA MWONGA

We met Caroline (Shiko) after starting the International Harvest Church in Euless, Texas, on October 10, 1999. Soon after, we were privileged to meet Caroline's parents, the Nkoyos. We got to know the Nkoyos and their God-given ability to be all things to all men. (The Nkoyos as a team could minister to any generation and to any culture.) The Nkoyos were guest speakers and participants during a marriage enrichment weekend seminar. They became a great blessing to many couples as they shared from their experience after years of marriage. We also discovered that the Rev. Mary Nkoyo had a passion for prayer and intercession. Many times while based in Irving, she would come by our church early in the morning just to pray for our congregation.

A few months before she went to be with the Lord, Mary walked into church early in the morning, but this time instead of praying as she usually did, she wanted to see the pastor to deliver a word that God had given her concerning our congregation. The word was that God would restore everything that the Devil had stolen. She encouraged us to maintain the momentum because the Lord had revealed to her that He would restore everything that we had lost. Sure enough, not long after that, we started witnessing that word being fulfilled. We thank God that Mary lived to the fullest and did not let physical challenges deter her from obeying God. She has left a great legacy to her family and to the body of Christ as a whole. She will always be in our hearts.

We miss Mary, but we are grateful that her memory and her legacy will live on within her family, her friends, and the community of faith. This tribute is no doubt the best way to honor the memory of the Rev. Mary Nkoyo, her family, her friends, and the community of faith that knew her labor of love in prayer and in action.

—Rev. Philip and Rebecca Mwonga,
Senior Pastors, International Harvest Church; married more than
twenty-five years

MAJ. (RETIRED) JOE GACHIE AND MRS. ROSE NJIRU

Major (Retired) and the late Mrs. Nkoyo turned out to be our closest family friends after we found each other in the great state of Texas. We often exchanged visits, burning the midnight oil talking about our children and our good old days in the military. Sometimes we mimicked our colleagues, producing waves of laughter that left our spouses and our children wondering what it was all about. But in the end, all this translated into a forum for moral, spiritual, and intellectual support of our families and into an enduring brotherly fellowship. We were always there for each other at family functions. We also discussed politics, economics, and general developments in our country, Kenya.

You did not need to look far to see evidence of the intense love this beautiful couple had for each other. They were most often found at each other's side. Of greater significance is the way this couple would look passionately and admiringly at each other and how one would speak as if speaking the other's mind.

Though we had been such great and long-term friends with the Nkoyos, it took a long time before we learned of Mary's health struggles. That was because of the way her husband so tenderly, lovingly, and compassionately handled her situation whenever she was down with depression. But in spite of her ailment, the Reverend Mary was a powerful woman of prayer and fully in charge of the International Prayer Network, a ministry she founded. She regularly organized prayer meetings that we and many others attended.

A Pictorial Story of Family in Phases Courtship, Marriage, Parenting and Grand parenting

Above: Wilfred Nkoyo converted to Christianity at age sixteen during his first year in secondary school (1970). He became a fiery evangelist and learned to played guitar and gospel music.

Below: Miss Mary Mbuthuri (left) at seventeen with her classmate and best friend, Martha Muigai, in Nyandarua secondary school (1971–74 before meeting Wilfred).

Below: Miss Mary Mbuthuri (right) with a friend in secondary school.

Above: Mary Mbuthuri, eighteen, in form four at Nyandarua High School soon after meeting and falling in love with Wilfred (May 1974). Note the penetrating eyes and the no-nonsense look.

Above: Mary Mbuthuri, twenty, with Nancy, a friend and classmate in form six at Nyandarua High School (1976). They were leaders of the Christian Union. Wilfred was an officer cadet in military college at the time.

Below: In high school, Wilfred and Mary spent most of their time together practicing gospel music for the Christian Union (1974–75) and on other gospel outreaches.

Below: Wilfred and Mary study and discuss Scripture in high school.

Below: Wilfred and Mary study and discuss Scripture in high school.

Above: Wilfred and Mary, the inseparable high school sweethearts (1974).

Above: Wilfred squatting and Mary (middle, standing) with other Christian Union leaders and school prefects in high school (1974–75). Mary wants to stand behind Wilfred, her favorite position, but brother Njeru won't let her and brother Kamau teases her. Sister Miriam, standing behind Mary, is fully and purposely eclipsed by Mary. (Wilfred was amused by the drama of Mary's obsession and by the significance of where she stood or sat in relation to him for the rest of her life.) In the background, the famous room where Mary told Wilfred, "Yes, I will." Their marriage came to pass five years later.

Below: Wilfred (right) preaching and Jeremiah (left) interpreting during a Narok crusade in 1974.

Below: Wilfred (front left) squatting and Mary (rear left) standing behind him, carrying his guitar. They are with the Narok evangelistic team on a December 1974 outreach in Maasai land.

Above: Mary in black (right) prepares to pray for conversion and other needs including healing of the sick during a Narok crusade in 1974. Evangelist Clement Kambo (Left)

Above: Mary in the middle with Beth (Wilfred's elder sister) and her daughter. Beth was one of our converts during the 1974 outreach in Maasai land.

Building a family and a military career (1977–88)
Maj. Wilfred Nkoyo and Mrs. Mary Nkoyo at the time of his retirement (1988).

Top: Deep in the jungle, Officer Cadet Nkoyo, as a radio operator
for his Platoon during training in jungle warfare (1976).
Bottom: Lieutenant Nkoyo in Mombasa city preparing for his honey
moon for upcoming wedding to Miss. Mary Mbuthuri (1979).

REPUBLIC OF KENYA

PRESIDENT'S COMMISSION

I, JOMO KENYATTA President and Commander-in-Chief of the Armed Forces of the Republic of Kenya, do give you ___Wilfred Robben Nkoyo___

greetings, and reposing especial trust and confidence in your loyalty, courage and good conduct, do by these presents constitute and appoint you to be an officer in the ___Kenya Armed Forces___ from the ___22nd___ day of ___April___, 19 ___77___. You are therefore carefully and diligently to discharge your duty as such in the rank of ___Second Lieutenant___ or in such other rank as I may from time to time hereafter promote or appoint you to, and you are in such manner and on such occasions as may be prescribed to exercise and well discipline in their duties such officers and men as may be placed under your orders. And I do hereby command them to obey you as their superior officer, and you to observe and follow such orders and directions as from time to time you shall receive from me, in pursuance of the trust hereby reposed in you.

GIVEN at Nairobi, this ___22nd___ day of ___April___, 1977.

_____
PRESIDENT

Above: A commission certificate and a special award presented to me personally by the president in recognition of my excellent performance in finishing at the top of a class of fifty with two other officer cadets in April 1977.

156

Top left: Lt. Wilfred Nkoyo and Miss Mary Mbuthuri during courtship (1977).

Top right: Lt. Wilfred Nkoyo in Nowshera, Pakistan, in 1978, attending military training and getting ready for his wedding in 1979. Bottom left: Miss Mary in a single room with Sister Anne Muthama in Nairobi, Kenya. Mary was working for an insurance firm in Nairobi in 1978 and faithfully preparing for her wedding on the return of the love of her life to Kenya.

Above: September 1979 was a memorable time because Wilfred and Mary got engaged in Nairobi. (That's Mary's little niece Wandia squatting.) Apostle Harry Das, founder of Crisco Churches, officiated at the colorful function attended by many relatives and friends in Nairobi.

Below: With clearly visible emotions and a
trembling hand, Brig. Dishon Mbuthuri, a
loving and caring father, walks his precious
daughter Mary to me to love and to hold.

Below: Pastor Joseck Mogotu
prays for the couple.

Above: Anxiously following events are Leah and
Onesmus Nkoyo, Wilfred's parents (front row
from right). Back row, left to right: Wilfred's
namesake grandfather and older brother Nathan.

Above: Wilfred and Mary
commit to the covenant, "Yes,
I do till death us part."

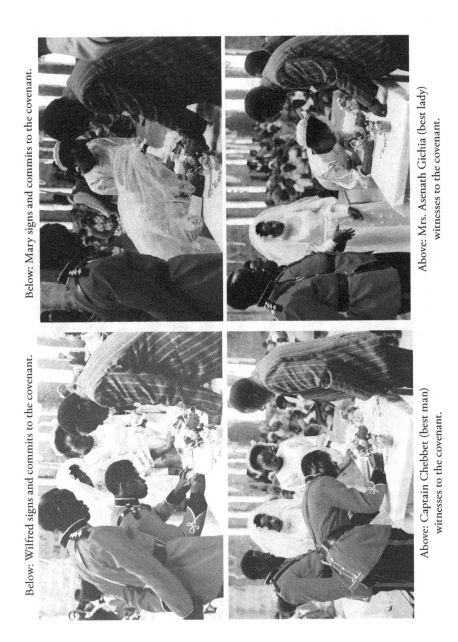

Below: Mary signs and commits to the covenant.

Above: Mrs. Asenath Gichia (best lady) witnesses to the covenant.

Below: Wilfred signs and commits to the covenant.

Above: Captain Chebbet (best man) witnesses to the covenant.

Below: Here is the covenant to uphold and to honor until death do us part.

Below: I, Wilfred, give to you, Mary, this ring as a symbol of my commitment to love, honor, and respect you until death do us part.

Above: I, Mary, give to you, Wilfred, this ring as a symbol of my commitment to love, honor, and respect you until death do us part.

Above: A commitment and a friendship that endured time and tests to the end whether in sickness or in health, in plenty or just enough.

Below: Emerging to military honors.

Below: An arc of swords and a sword on my waist with special meaning: "Committed and sworn to protect Mary my bride at any cost all my life."

Above: Marching off into a future of honour.

Above: Mrs. Mary Nkoyo is inducted into a military family of honour.

Above: Accreditation to the US army and similarly to air force and navy while serving as an assistant military attaché of Kenyan armed forces based at the Kenyan embassy in Washington, D.C. (1982–84).

163

Below: Mary at home in Washington, D.C., caring for our two adorable kids, Caroline and Armstrong.

Below: Captain Nkoyo in the Washington, D.C., office attending to a military student (1983).

Above: Captain Nkoyo (right) visiting a Kenyan military student at a military special training institution in northern Virginia, USA (1983).

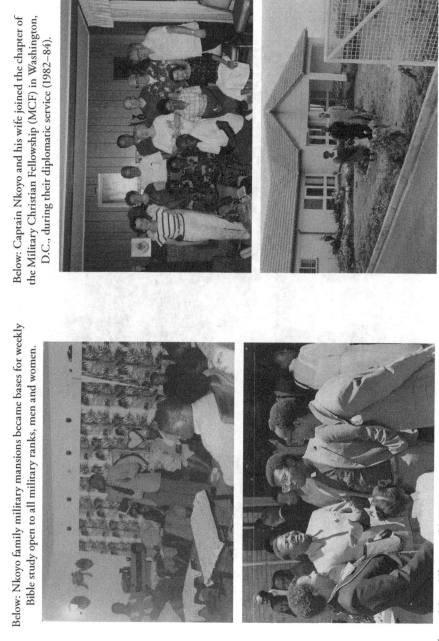

Below: Captain Nkoyo and his wife joined the chapter of the Military Christian Fellowship (MCF) in Washington, D.C., during their diplomatic service (1982–84).

Above: Captain Nkoyo and his wife hosting missionary friends of different nationalities. (Seen above, Brother Hans from Sweden)

Below: Nkoyo family military mansions became bases for weekly Bible study open to all military ranks, men and women.

Above: Major Nkoyo and his wife chat with delegates from African countries outside an MCF international conference in Nairobi (1986).

Above: Major Nkoyo and his wife prepare daughter Caroline to present a bouquet to the president and commander in chief during an MCF conference in 1986.

Above: The Nkoyo family (Captain Nkoyo holding daughter Caroline, three, and
Mary holding Armstrong, one) in Washington, D.C., in the fall of 1983.

Below: Mary and Wilfred with Caroline and Armstrong in Nakuru, Kenya, after returning from a diplomatic mission in 1984.

Above: Wilfred and his two children say good-bye to Kaptagat Preparatory School pupils and staff on their way to the United States in 1992.

Below: The Nkoyo family visiting Margaret and Sid Williams, family friends, in Fredericksburg, Virginia (1983).

Above: Mary and the kids visit with her family in Gilgil in 1986. The children meet their maternal grandparents uncles and aunts.

Above left: Our first rental home in a Limuru tea plantation where I pitched the first ministry tent (top right) for Mary to launch a women's ministry for home care fellowship and where we hosted Christians retreating for prayers and fasting.

Above bottom: The veranda of our second home (a five-minute walk from the first, above left) where we were brutally attacked in 1990.

Top left: The four human angels we hosted, who represented God's intervention on behalf of our family during the night of terror.

Top right: A sample of the twenty-one windows and eight doors knocked down on the night of terror.

Bottom left: A welding crew reinstalling the metal frame and grill on the window that the thugs demolished in attempting to enter our stronghold. At this window I shot one "super" arrow that stopped the multitude.

Above: It was all joy in the morning after a night of terror. Thanks to God for His mighty intervention. The Nkoyo family—Caroline, ten; Wilfred, Mary, and Armstrong, eight—survived unscathed except for the wound on my eyebrow. To the right, a grill barely hangs on the window through which gang members tried to enter until a super-charged arrow shot stopped them.

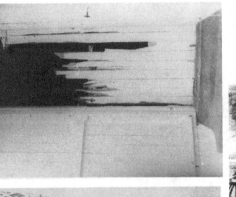

Above left: The godsend angels (standing left to right): brother Rukenya, brother Mathenge, name forgotten, and brother Otieno.

Top right: The wooden door slashed to the bottom with machetes and knocked off the hinges (replaced temporarily for the photograph).

Bottom right: The drawer cabinet, a gift from our wedding in 1979, by divine provision became our shield (flipped on its side to cover part of the open doorway after the door was knocked out) on the night of terror.

The tent ministry: Christian Heritage Ministries International (CHMI Inc.), which started outside our homestead in Limuru in December 1989, soon grew into a huge tent outreach extending to different parts of the country and bringing the message of healing and salvation to many who thronged the tent grounds. Our tents could seat as many as two thousand.

Scenes from tent ministry outreach.

The CHMI tent ministry organizers and prayer partners. From left, evangelist Akilimali Balagizi, Pastor Jack Kariuki, evangelist Wilfred Nkoyo, and evangelist Mary Nkoyo getting ready for action during the Gilgil outreach in 1989.

Above: Mary Nkoyo
ministers in music.

Above: Our evangelistic band.

Above: One cripple healed and
many respond in Gilgil town.

Above: And many responded
to the call to salvation.

Above: Evangelist Mary Nkoyo invites the crowds to come to Jesus. The
passion, the confidence, and the faith are evident in the accompanying joy.
(Gilgil is Mary's hometown and last military base served).

Left: Caroline (two years, four months) in Washington, D.C., in 1983.

Top right: Caroline's first day at preschool in Washington, D.C. (October 1983).

Bottom right: Caroline, twelve, with classmates at Kaptagat Preparatory School, Kenya, where she competed against boys, who traditionally dominated the first ten class positions. She ended up third from the top just before leaving for the United States (1992).

Above left: Mary Nkoyo, a frugal mother shopping for her family. Center and right: Caroline during her Mount Vernon High School years with a nurturing and loving mother who molded her into the woman, mother, and wife she is today, modelling decency and faithfulness for her daughter.

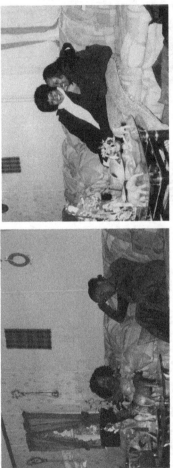

Above left: Tough love for a daughter by a caring mother. Above right: Ladies-only day, a time for mother-daughter bonding between Mary and Caroline.

Left: Caroline graduates from Mount Vernon High School in the Gifted and Talented Student program (1998).
Top right: Caroline, a high school senior, buys one car (a red Chrysler) with her savings from a job. She gets another (a blue Pontiac) from proud parents to take to Baylor University where she was admitted for pre-med in 1999.
Bottom right: Caroline in the 1998 yearbook at Mount Vernon High School in Alexandria, Virginia.

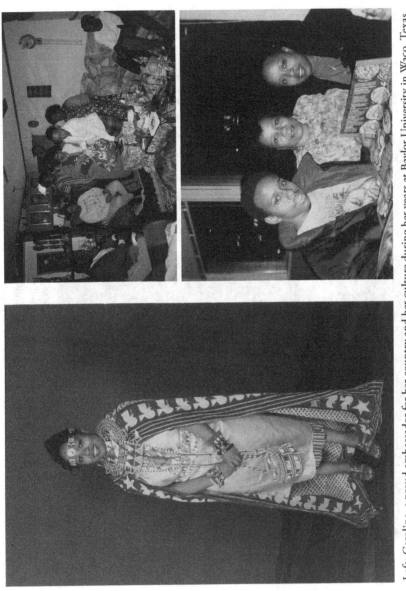

Left: Caroline, a proud ambassador for her country and her culture during her years at Baylor University in Waco, Texas.
Top right: Caroline receives gifts during a send-off to college by proud parents and family friends. Bottom right: Mother and her teens eat out—a special treat. "I just want you both to know how proud you make me and your dad for the positive choices you make daily."

Left: Caroline proudly displays her diploma after graduating with a pre-med degree from Baylor University in Waco, Texas (2004). Top right: Caroline's parents relocated from Alexandria, Virginia, to Waco, Texas, in 2001 to be close to her and to proudly celebrate with her after her graduation from Baylor University.

Caroline does it again, receiving her diploma after graduating with a master's degree from Emory University in Georgia in 2006. Top left and right: Caroline, family, and friends have a moment of pride.

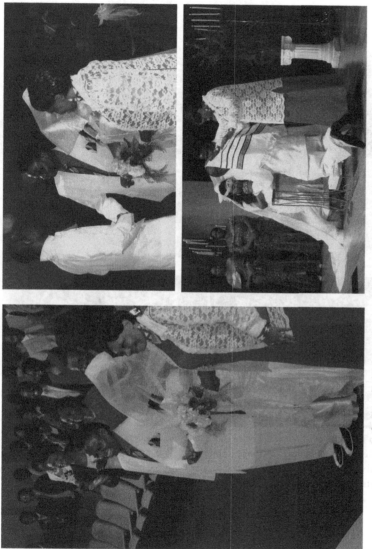

Left: Proud and happy parents walk their only daughter to her groom.
Top right: A proud couple trustingly hands over Caroline to Daniel.
Bottom right: "Under this prayer shawl, this symbolic tent of meeting, you will call upon the name of the Lord to supply all your needs. And, in your marriage wilderness walks, this Bible, never to leave your side as your road map. The Holy Spirit be your guide and compass. Amen!"

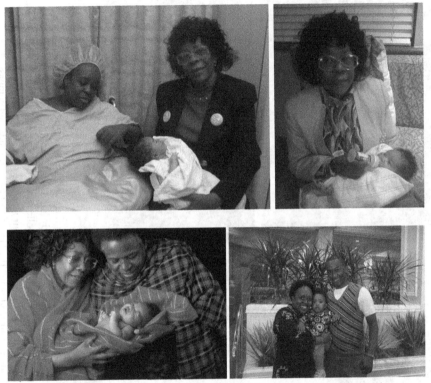

Top left and right: Mary, a loving mother, defied her doctor's advice, and travelled to Georgia despite kidney failure to be by her daughter's side during delivery of her first baby and stayed to help until the baby was a year old.
Bottom left: Proud grandparents admiring their grandbaby, only a couple of days old.
Bottom right: Daniel's family.

Left: Armstrong at about four months old in Washington, D.C.
Top right: Armstrong, one, at home with a nurturing mother in Washington, D.C.
Bottom right: Armstrong at eight in Tigoni Primary
School, Kenya (after our night of terror).

Below left: Armstrong in the yearbook at Rolling Valley Elementary School in Springfield, Virginia, his first encounter with computer technology (1993). Below right: Armstrong, mama's boy at the annual CPT camp meeting USA in Ashland, Virginia, in 1994.

Below left: Armstrong, a thirteen-year-old computer whiz kid at Walt Whitman Middle School (1995). Below right: Mama's not happy with teen son, now fourteen. "Armstrong, you missed the school bus. You have no reason. This is a habit. Get up now and walk to school. I will not drive you there."

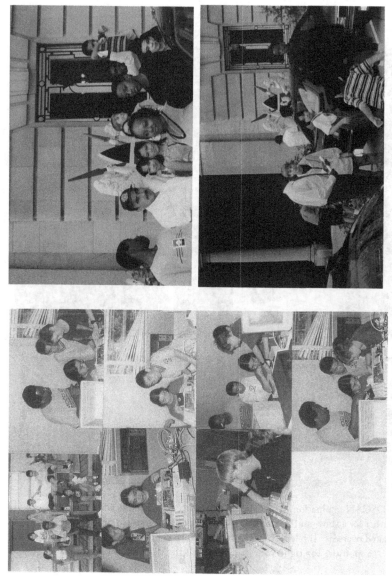

Left: Scenes of the KIDSCAN program in Alexandria, Virginia, during its early stages. It outgrew the allocated trailer after Armstrong and his buddies came on board. Right top and bottom: Kids visit the Kenyan Embassy in Washington, D.C., during a tour of institutions. Caroline volunteers to participate to help control the kids.

KIDSCAN graduation day at a hotel conference hall. Parents and sponsors gather for a show-and-tell on how old computers are restored by kids and donated overseas. Top left: The Rev. Mary Nkoyo confers with Jo Gummelt, a sponsor. Top right: Mary video records the show for ministry.

Top left: Armstrong at about seventeen, now trouble-free, has a
job and laughs with amusement about his earlier years.
Top right: Armstrong's yearbook picture from his senior
year at Mount Vernon High School.
Bottom right: The family hangs out during Armstrong's
time at Texas State Technical College.

Below left and right: Armstrong graduates from Texas State Technical College with a proud family on hand.

Above left: Armstrong's first home of his own. Right: Armstrong earns a degree in business.

190

Top left: Armstrong meets his soul mate Jerusha. Top center and left: Preparations for Armstrong's wedding at the family mansion in Waco. Bottom left: The couple saying "I do" at a wedding house in Waco before Pastor Kimathi of Dallas Presbyterian Church. Bottom right: Armstrong and Jerusha are declared husband wife in July 2011.

op left and center: Armstrong and his brand-new bride, Jerusha Nkoyo.
Top right: Armstrong shows off his bride. Bottom left: Signing the covenant. Bottom right: The newlyweds with both families. The two are off to a new life after crossing the suspension bridge in Waco, Texas.

Top left: Mary was admitted to Parkland Hospital in Dallas and missed the wedding in Waco. Here a reenactment is done at the hospital in her honor. The bride is given to us by an aunt.

Top right: Mary kisses her son's bride to say, "Welcome home."

Bottom left: A proud mother kisses her son. Bottom right: Proud parents of the new couple.

Top left: At Parkland Hospital, Mary and I declare blessings upon our newly wedded son and his wife. Bottom left: Proud parents of John born in August 2014. Bottom right: A proud grandpa bottle feeding John in the home office.

Above left: Attending the annual Calvary Pentecostal Tabernacle camp meeting, where our new life in America began in September 1992, on invitation by the Rev. Heflin Wallace, camp director.

Top right: Wilfred Nkoyo ordained and Mary licensed as ministers of the gospel at Good Samaritan Church in Suitland, Maryland (1994).

Mid-right: The Nkoyo family ministers in music at a church with daughter Caroline joining.

Bottom right: In Alexandria, Virginia, celebrating their nineteenth anniversary in 1998, Wilfred tries Mary-taught tambourine skills. Mary was always keen on marking anniversaries and birthdays and always dressed appropriately.

Top left: Ordination of the Rev. Mary Nkoyo by Bishop, now Dr. Canon, John Kivuva at the Word of Life Assembly of God in Springfield, Virginia, in 1996.

Top right: The Rev. Mary Nkoyo ministering at one of her monthly meetings in a hotel ballroom (1996). Bottom left: Mary Nkoyo poses with Mary Ford, her ministry supporter and our first host in Springfield, Virginia, from 1992 to 1994. Bottom right: Reverend Mary (left with hat) poses with ladies during a KCFF conference organized by the Rev. Anne Muthama to which she was invited as one of the guest speakers.

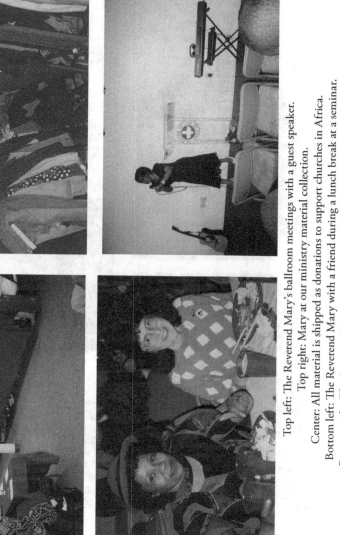

Top left: The Reverend Mary's ballroom meetings with a guest speaker.
Top right: Mary at our ministry material collection.
Center: All material is shipped as donations to support churches in Africa.
Bottom left: The Reverend Mary with a friend during a lunch break at a seminar.
Bottom right: The Reverend Mary in action, preaching in a church in Waco, Texas.

Above: Views of our mansion in Waco, Texas, during its dedication for ministry work in 2010. Dr. Rev. Joe Njoroge and his wife, the Rev. Margret from Georgia, officiated, and many partners from Texas graced the occasion.

Above: On this colorful occasion in November 2013, family and friends of the Rev. Mary Nkoyo celebrated her fifty-eighth birthday at All Nations Church in Irving, Texas, during her last International Prayer Network meeting. The event marked her last birthday, her last ministry activity with the whole family in attendance, and her final "summation" sermon, "The anointing of God will open doors for you."

Below: Caroline poses with the mother she tenderly watched and nursed 24/7 in the ICU to the last day.

Above: Following passionate speeches about the Reverend Mary by ministers and speakers during the fundraising/memorial service at All Nations Church, Irving, Texas.

Below: The Reverend Mary in the Baylor ICU surrounded by her loving family during visiting hours. It was all family fun and jokes.

Above: Gospel ministers from the Dallas-Fort Worth area gathered for Mary's memorial service at All Nations Church.

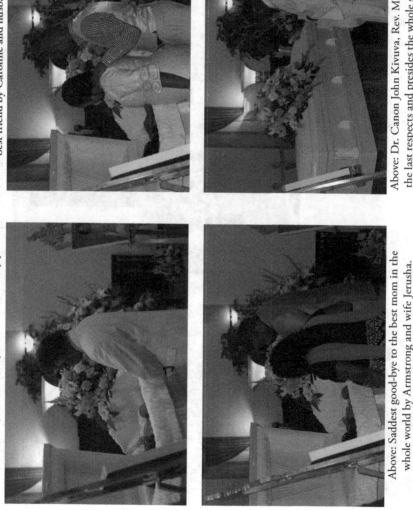

Below: Saddest good-bye to a model mother and best friend by Caroline and husband Daniel.

Above: Dr. Canon John Kivuva, Rev. Mary's Bishop pays the last respects and presides the whole service for Mary.

Below: Saddest moment, saying good-bye to the queen of my heart, my love, and my best friend of forty years.

Above: Saddest good-bye to the best mom in the whole world by Armstrong and wife Jerusha.

Above: Scenes from the funeral home during the memorial service for Mary. The presiding bishop, Dr. Canon John Kivuva (Mary's bishop, inset), turned a time of mourning and sadness into a moment of celebration, telling many memorable humorous stories about Mary and the Nkoyo family. Top right: Mary's elder sister Elizabeth gave a moving and passionate speech about her life with Mary and the Nkoyo family.

Top left: Caroline and husband Daniel speak at the funeral service. Top right: Pastor Lucy Kingori (author of the foreword) delivers the eulogy at the service. Bottom left: Wilfred Nkoyo sings in honor of his wife. Bottom right: Armstrong and wife Jerusha speak during the service.

Below: In a hearse on the last ride with my love.

Below: The plot marker.

Bluebonnet Hills
FUNERAL HOME • CEMETERY

M. Nkoyo

SERVICE

Above: Standing together as one, the Nkoyo family and our closest relatives escort our hero and pride to her resting place. This was the greatest honor we could give to Mary, whose life was all about love of God, family, and friends.

Above: Armstrong, Daniel, Pastor Karari (Mary's nephew), and close family friends proudly bear the remains of their hero to her final resting place.

Below: The Nkoyo family and relatives.

Below: The Nkoyo and Daniel families listen to speeches.

Above: The Nkoyo family and friends join in singing and in praising God at the funeral.

Above: Nkoyo family friends from across the United States and elsewhere in the world join in prayer during the funeral.

Above left: The larger Nkoyo family, with aunts, uncles, nephews, nieces, and grannies, in America. Above right: The core family, with Dr. Canon John Kivuva and Mr. Thungu (Mary's cousin). Bottom left: Mary's children and spouses: Armstrong and wife Jerusha, and Daniel and wife Caroline (the Nkoyos' daughter).

We Remain As One to the End

In the beginning, there were two Nkoyos—two in the shadows—but we stood as one. Then there were three—one in the shadows—but we still stood as one. And then there were four standing strong as one.

Here, we are back to three—one in the shadows—but we remain as one, rejoicing in the Lord that whether we were two, three, four, or back to three, tough time or good times, trials or triumphs, nothing could separate us, neither death nor life. Things that are or things that are to come shall never separate us from the love of God and the love and commitment to each other or our friends. As we stood strong together in all things so shall we remain strong as one to the end of life on this side of heaven. Amen

Above, from right to left: Wilfred Nkoyo and children Caroline, Daniel and Armstrong.

My Mom, My Beautiful Rose That Never Faded or Fell

I now return to Georgia, where I left in a hurry, leaving everything that is dear to me—my family, home, and work—to come and be by your side, you who bore me and nurtured me into what I am today. But little did I know that was to become the most precious last week in more than thirty-four years or that I was going to be by your bedside 24/7. I now take with me these two fresh roses from where we laid you to rest, honoring the last words you spoke to me minutes before you passed saying, "I am tired. I want to rest." Let the beauty of one of these roses represent all the past with a beautiful mom who lived out her life as my model of excellence: a faithful and loving wife to my father, a dear mother to me and my brother, a grandmother to our children, an exemplary minister of good news, and a friend of many. Let the beauty of this second rose represent the future full of hope and determination for me as I try to emulate everything womanly you exemplified for me as your daughter, watching you from when I was a little girl and dreaming that one day I would become like you. These roses will soon fade and fall, but one thing I am certain is that you have pioneered again for us into a land where roses never fade or fall and so will the true meaning of these two roses never fade or fall from my heart. Rest in peace my sweet mom and best friend, till we meet again in that land where we will never part again.

Above: Caroline reflections

208

Above: I point out to my children, Caroline and Armstrong, with
Dr. Canon John Kivuva looking on as a witness, where I must be laid
when I pass on from this life—side by side with my love.

Above (left to right):Daniel and family, myself and Armstrong
and family in Georgia for Christmas 2014.

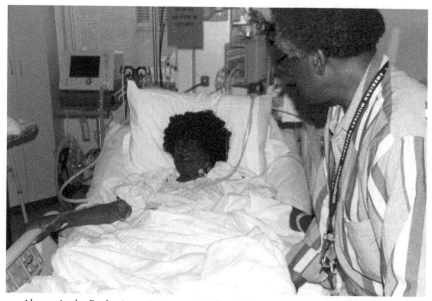

Above: At the Baylor intensive care unit where Mary spent her last week of life, I am seen helping her turn on her side for comfort. Mary left for eternity surrounded by family. During the short time when she could not verbalize her adoration, whenever I entered her room, her blood pressure and heart rate would normalize and her face would glow with life, joy, and hope. A smile would come to her lips, and her eyes would sparkle, overflowing with love and admiration (as seen in the picture on the inside of the front cover). All of this took place to the consternation of nurses, doctors, her older sister Elizabeth, and our children. Mary would turn her head in the direction of my voice and gaze at me with wonderment as I walked toward her bed.

About the Author

Wilfred R. Nkoyo, a retired major of the Kenyan army, was born on July 14, 1954. After graduating from secondary school in Narok, Kenya, in 1973, he went on for advanced levels at Nyandarua High School (1974–75) where he met his future wife, Miss. Mary Mbuthuri. In 1976, he became an officer cadet at the Kenyan Armed Forces Training College, graduating on April 22, 1977. His Excellency Jomo Kenyatta, Kenya President and Commander In Chief commissioned him as an officer in the army. During his twelve years as a combat and staff officer, Nkoyo received extensive training and served in different capacities, including as an assistant military attaché in Washington, D.C., from 1982 to 1984. In October 1979, as an army Lieutenant he got married to his high school sweetheart Mrs. Mary Nkoyo.

In August 1988, Nkoyo retired from the army so that he and his wife could get more involved in Christian evangelism, a passion dating back to their high school days. They also wanted to start vocational training projects to help equip young people with the skills for self-advancement. In 1992, Nkoyos decided to return to United States of America with their two little children, Caroline and Armstrong. Wilfred and Mary entered the National Bible Institute in Maryland to study Theology. After graduating, he was ordained as a minister of the gospel in 1995. Wilfred and Mary are experts on youth redemptive interventions and spent years working with troubled, abused, and abandoned youths of all ages from many nations, helping them to reconnect with society and to find purpose in life. From 2001 to 2008, he and his wife worked with the Methodist Children's Home in Waco, Texas, and with the Baptist Children's Home in Round Rock, Texas, as home parents.

Married for thirty-five years (1979-2014), the author and his late wife became popular speakers in churches on marriage relationships and counseled youth, families and couples in troubled marriages. Their children, Caroline, thirty-four, and Armstrong, thirty-two are both married. He is also a grandfather of two. Major (Retired) Nkoyo is enrolled with the

American Military University, pursuing a degree in International Relations and majoring in Globalization and Human Security. An American citizen, he lives in Waco, Texas. He is a fervent advocate and a solid role model for strong marriage commitments and positive parenting.